Sex After Sixty

*A Guide for Men and Women
for Their Later Years*

Robert N. Butler, M.D.

and

Myrna I. Lewis, ACSW

G.K.HALL &CO.

 Boston, Massachusetts

1977

Library of Congress Cataloging in Publication Data

Butler, Robert N
  Sex after sixty.

  Large print ed.
  Bibliography: p.
  Includes index.
  1. Aged—Psychology. 2. Sex (Psychology)
I. Lewis, Myrna I., joint author. II. Title
[BF724.85.S48B87 1977] 301.41'8 77-12151
ISBN 0-8161-6507-6

Published in Large Print by arrangement with Harper & Row, Publishers

Set in Compugraphic 18 pt English Times

Contents

Acknowledgments

A number of colleagues in the medical field have read portions of this book in manuscript, and we want to acknowledge gratefully the help of Dr. Leslie Libow, internist (New York, N.Y.), Dr. William T. Bowles, urologist (St. Louis, Mo.), Dr. Theodore G. Duncan, endocrinologist (Philadelphia, Pa.), Dr. Julius Fogel, gynecologist (Washington, D.C.), Dr. Constance Friess, internist (New York, N.Y.), Dr. Robert B. Greenblatt, endocrinologist (Augusta, Ga.), Dr. Raymond Harris, cardiologist (Albany, N.Y.), Dr. John C. Kinealy, urologist (Washington, D.C.), and Dr. Manuel Rodstein, cardiologist (New York, N.Y.).

Professor Marjorie Fiske Lowenthal of the University of California (San Francisco), Margaret Kuhn of the Gray Panthers, and Irina Posner of CBS News's *Magazine* reviewed the manuscript. The authors are of course entirely responsible for any statements in the book with which individual consultants may not agree.

We are grateful to David Bress and Newton Frohlich for their assistance in legal matters; Jean Jones of the American Psychiatric Association and John Balkema of the National Council on the Aging for library research; and Thomas A. Ziebarth, attorney of the Consumer Protection Office of the U.S. Postal Service, for information he kindly provided. The evidence of sexual desire and activity among older people is available in the original data of the National Institute of Mental Health's study on *Human Aging* (1955 - 1962) in which Robert N. Butler participated. Monte Vanness and Cindy Hamilton were able typists of the manuscript through its several drafts.

We especially thank Ann Harris, our

editor at Harper & Row, for her
constructive and sensitive guidance and
criticism.

Sex After Sixty

Every day five thousand Americans turn sixty. Altogether thirty million people, or one out of every seven of us, is sixty or older. What happens to sex at this time of life? Many persons — not only the young and the middle-aged but older people themselves — simply assume that it is over. This is nonsense. Our own clinical and research work, the work of other gerontologists, the research of Kinsey and the clinical discoveries of Masters and Johnson all demonstrate that relatively healthy older people who enjoy sex are capable of experiencing it — often until *very* late in life. Those who do have sexual problems can frequently be helped.

We have written this book for those older men and women who are presently or potentially interested in sex — as well as for younger people who wish to understand their elders better or want to prepare for their own later lives. We will offer solutions to sexual problems that may occur and propose means for countering negative attitudes that older people may experience — within themselves, from family members, from the medical and psychotherapeutic professions, and from society at large. We especially want older people to know that their feelings and problems are not unique, that they are not alone in their experience, and that many others feel exactly as they do. Even those people who have had a lively enthusiasm and capacity for sex all their lives often need information, support and sometimes various kinds of treatment in order to continue sexual activity as the years go by. In addition, people for whom sex may not have been especially satisfying in their younger days may find that it is possible to improve its quality despite long-standing difficulties.

Sex and sexuality are pleasurable, rewarding and fulfilling experiences that enhance the later years. They are also — as everyone knows — enormously complex psychologically. Every one of us carries with us throughout our lives a weight of infant and childhood experiences related to sex that have been shaped by ourselves, our parents, our families, our teachers and our society, some of which are positive and some negative, some of which we realize and many of which we are unaware of.

Because of this, it is useful to understand what underlies so many of the attitudes and problems about sex that one encounters. If you are an older person who is interested in sex, be prepared for the likelihood of conflicting feelings within yourself and contradictory attitudes from the outside world. Should older people have sex lives? Are they able to make love? Do they really want to? Is it appropriate — that is, "normal" or "decent" — or is sexual interest a sign of "senility" and brain disease (he/she has gone "daft"), poor judgment or an

3

embarrassing inability to adjust to aging with proper restraint and resignation?

How much less troubling it would be to accept the folklore of cookie-baking grandmothers who bustle about the kitchen making goodies for their loved ones while rocking-chair grandfathers puff on their pipes and reminisce. Idealized folk figures like these are not supposed to have sex lives of their own. After all, they are our parents and grandparents, not ordinary adults with the same needs and desires that we have.

As an older man or woman you may find that love and sex in later life, when they are acknowledged at all, will be patronizingly thought of as "cute" or "sweet," like the puppy love of teen-agers; but the odds are that they will be ridiculed, a subject for jokes that have undercurrents of disdain and apprehensiveness at the prospect of growing older. Mother-in-law jokes and stories follow women from middle age into old age. St. Petersburg, Florida, where many older people live, has been called a "pooped-out Peyton Place." Our language is full of telltale phrases: older men become "dirty old men," "old fools" or "old goats" where sex is involved. Older women are depicted as "biddies," "hags" and "crocks." Most of this "humor" implies the impotence of older men and the assumed ugliness of older women.

A mythology fed by misinformation surrounds late-life sexuality. The presumption is that sexual desire automatically ebbs with age — that it begins to decline when one is in one's forties, proceeds relentlessly downward (you are "failing fast") and eventually hits bottom (you are "over the hill") at some time between sixty and sixty-five. Thus an older woman who shows an evident, perhaps even a lusty, interest in sex is often assumed to be suffering from "emotional" problems; and if she is obviously in her right mind and sexually active, she runs the risk of being called "depraved" or, more kindly, said to be clinging pathetically to her lost youth.

Lustiness in young men is called lechery in older men. Those men who do manage to conduct themselves in a way that wins grudging admiration from their peers, and from those who are younger, escape with the relatively mild appelation of "rake" or "roué." An older man's show of affection toward children other than his own grandchildren or those of his friends is greeted with suspicion, as though this automatically had a sexual tinge. "Child molesting" is popularly associated with older men, although it is a crime committed primarily by young men with an average age of twenty-seven. Older women are permitted more latitude in expressing affection for children because they are seen as motherly rather than seductive.

From time to time everybody is caught up by accounts of older people who perform sexual feats "despite" their age. Newspapers relish them: "92-year-old man is father of twins"; "Woman of 73 and man of 76 arrested by police in love nest"; "Judge of 81 marries 22-year-old showgirl"; "72-year-old woman jailed for attempted prostitution." In the popular mind these older people walk the thin line between sexual heroics and indecency, with part of the public saying "More power to them" and the remainder reacting with disgust. Everyone, however, reads the accounts with the mixture of revulsion and fascination reserved for the extraordinary and the bizarre.

Why are we so negative about sex in later life and about older people in general? Much of this attitude, of course, is an outgrowth of our own fear of growing old and dying, and it has given rise to a prejudice we have called *ageism,* which is systematic discrimination against people because they are old, just as racism and sexism discriminate for reasons of skin color and gender. The ageist sees older people in stereotypes: rigid, boringly talkative, senile, old-fashioned in morality and lacking in skills, useless and with little redeeming social value. There's a fine irony in the fact that if the ageists live long enough they are going to end up being "old" themselves and the victims, in turn, of their own prejudice. When this realization penetrates, these attitudes can turn into self-hatred. A great many older people have fallen into this trap, often at devastating cost to their personal happiness. As far as sexuality is concerned, ageism is largely a matter of desexualization in its ultimate form: if you are getting old, you're finished.

Some of these attitudes have roots in memories of a relatively recent past. At the turn of the century, when the average life expectancy was forty-seven years, few older people lived to old age and fewer still were healthy enough to be sexually active. But today life expectancy is seventy-one years and we have a large population of relatively healthy people over sixty-five. Ninety-five percent of them live in the community, 81 percent can get around by themselves, and 30 percent are still working. (We now term the age period 65 - 74 "early old age," and call those over seventy-five in "later old age.") We have not accepted these new realities, however, nor have popular attitudes caught up; the general image of late life still assumes frailty or decrepitude.

If we join these cultural attitudes with

the prevalent sexual "yardsticks" by which we are all influenced, it is no wonder that older people may be confused and uncertain about sex. Both men and women worry about "wearing out" physically. They want to know what changes are to be expected with normal aging, whether there is reasonable hope for a physically healthy and active sex life, and whether sex can be as good as it was when they were younger.

Men are special victims of a lifelong excessive emphasis on physical performance. Masculinity is equated with physical prowess. Older men judge themselves and are judged by comparing the frequency and potency of their sexual performance with that of younger men. These comparisons seldom place any value on experience and on the quality of sex. When measured by standards that are essentially athletic, older men are naturally considered inferior. They often panic at the first sign of change: "Lately I've been troubled by the fact that I seem to take longer to have a good erection. Is this a sign that something is wrong? Am I becoming impotent?" They do not know what further changes may lie ahead. "Will I be able to have a firm erection as I get older?" they ask. "Will my penis stay hard long enough to give my partner pleasure and to give me an ejaculation? Will my ejaculations be as pleasurable as when I was younger?"

Women are under less pressure in terms of performance, of course, but they, too, worry about changes. They may report they are losing their "grip," namely the muscle strength in the vagina that enables them to hold a penis. The size of the vagina itself may change, and there may be problems with "dryness" as vaginal lubrication lessens. Some women begin to experience pain during intercourse and want to know what to do to eliminate it.

But the predominant pressure on women comes from what can be termed "aesthetic narrowness," that widespread assumption that only the young are beautiful. Many older people believe this themselves. When women's hair turns gray, and their skins develop wrinkles and their bodies lose their earlier firmness and suppleness, they are very likely to see themselves as unattractive. The idea of beauty needs more sophisticated redefinition so that it includes character, intelligence, expressiveness, knowledge, achievement, disposition, tone of voice and speech patterns, posture and bearing, warmth, personal style, social skills — all those personal traits that make each individual unique and that can be found at any age.

In late life we find just as many complaints between partners about sexual incompatibilities as at any other time: interest on one side and disinterest on the other, or passivity, or rebuffs, or failure to agree on frequency. Problems also arise between couples when one partner is incapacitated or chronically ill and the other is healthy. If the healthy partner has active sexual needs, anger and irritation often lead to guilt, as if one were lacking the appropriate concern and compassion for the ailing partner. The latter, in turn, may feel guilty at being unable to participate in love-making.

Tension in the later years often arises when those who are parents are inhibited by sons and daughters who find it uncomfortable to accept sexuality in their mothers and fathers. (We all know that, God forbid, *our* parents were not interested in sex!) Many adults continue to be bound by a primitive childhood need to deny their parents a sex life and to lock them into purely parental roles. For these children their parents are never fellow adults. Nor are the motivations always psychological. Avarice and selfishness are, unhappily, common. If one parent dies, children may try to prevent the surviving parent from meeting new friends (and potential new partners) in order to protect their inheritance. Any evidence of parental sexuality or romance threatens them.

We have been sketching a number of ways — positive and negative — in which individuals and society react to sex in older people. But what if you are not particularly interested in sex? Sizable numbers of older people feel this way. We want to emphasize that sexual disinterest is a matter of concern only if you find it personally troubling or if it causes problems in relating to others. Certain older people never were significantly interested in sex even as young people, whether because of biological makeup or, more often, as a result of social conditioning. For others sex has been a long-standing focus of emotional conflict resulting from or causing difficult relations with their partners. For them and their partners the opportunity to discontinue sex under the socially acceptable guise of "sexless old age" can be a great relief.

There are others who have simply grown tired of sex. It may have been shared with the same partner routinely for many years, and they have compensated for its dullness by developing satisfying nonsexual activities. Other people may have stopped sex because of disabilities or serious illnesses. When their health improved there was often no motivation to change what had become a comfortable habit. Sometimes an individual will have made a deliberate decision to share sex only with a particular partner, and when illness or death intervened, sex ended. Other people view sex only for procreation, not pleasure, and feel their religion supports this conviction, so sex ends with the completion of menopause. Self-imposed abstinence from sex may also be the continuation of a lifelong habit. This can often be traced back to frightening early experiences or to feelings that sex is forbidden and dangerous, and the avoidance of sex altogether may provide an adjustment that works reasonably well.

Whatever the reasons, it is possible to live a happy and satisfying life without sex if that is one's choice, and a good many older people do exactly that. America's emphasis on sexuality tends to make even young people feel guilty, inadequate or incomplete if sex fails to play a central role in their lives, and we certainly do not want to place a similar pressure on older persons. It cannot be said too strongly that those who have neither a desire for nor an interest in sex, or who have deliberately chosen a life style in which sexuality plays little or no part, have a right to their decision. Each of us is entitled to live the life he or she finds most fulfilling.

On the other hand, those older people who do enjoy sex deserve encouragement and support, as well as necessary information and appropriate treatment if problems arise. Sexuality, the physical and emotional responsiveness to sexual stimuli, goes beyond the sex urge and the sex act. For many older people it offers the opportunity to express not only passion but affection, esteem and loyalty. It provides affirmative evidence that one can count on one's body and its functioning. It allows people to assert themselves positively. It carries with it the possibility of excitement and romance. It expresses delight in being alive. It offers a continuous challenge to grow and change in new directions.

2

Normal Physical Changes in Sex and Sexuality with Age

What happens to your body sexually as it ages? There are significant changes in the physical and physiological aspects of sex with age, but, in the absence of disease or adverse drug effects, such changes do not usually cause sexual problems.

The act of sex is complex, encompassing the body, the mind and the emotions. The physiology of sex includes nervous system and hormonal activity as well as specific organs of the body. All these are involved in the sex act, which has four phases: the excitement or erotic-arousal phase; the intromission or plateau phase (in which the penis is placed in the vagina); the orgasmic or climax phase; and the resolution or recovery phase. This is called the sexual-response cycle. Essentially the same phases hold true for both men and women. People are stimulated sexually in a number of ways — through sight, smell, touch, thoughts and feelings. The pelvic area reacts. Muscle tension and congestion (filling of the blood vessels) occur, especially in the sexual or genital organs.

Sex hormones play an active role in this responsiveness. (A hormone is a chemical substance produced by a gland and discharged directly into the blood stream, where it is carried to certain organs and affects the activity of these organs.) Sex hormones, which are chemically steroids, are produced in the adrenal glands of both men and women, and in the ovaries of women and the testes of men. Estrogen is one of the active female hormones and has a profound effect on the generative organs and breasts of women; the functions of androgen, the primary male hormone, are less well understood. Hormone levels are influenced by the pituitary gland in the brain, the body's master gland. This very complex system operates in a relatively unchanging manner until the later years.

Older Women

Older women experience little deterioration in the physical *capacity* for sex as they age. We know more about the sexual situation of aging women than that of aging men because we understand more about the role of female hormones in sexuality than we do about male hormones. Most of the sexual changes in women can be directly traced to the decline of female hormones (such as estrogen) following menopause, rather than to "aging" itself. Menopause, also called the "change of life" or "climacteric," is a physiological process which continues for several years, anywhere between ages thirty-five and fifty-five, but usually between forty-five and fifty, with fluctuations in estrogen levels from normal to near zero. Its most conspicuous sign is the cessation of menstruation.

The menopause is a rich source of old wives' tales about insanity, the loss of sexual desire and attractiveness, the inevitability of depression, the occurrence of severe physical symptoms and masculinization. Actually, 60 percent of all women experience no remarkable physical or emotional symptoms with menopause, and most of those who do, experience only minimal to moderate physical problems. Symptoms resulting from hormonal imbalance may include hot flashes, headaches and neckaches, excessive fatigue and feelings of emotional instability. None of these are inevitable, and when they do occur, they usually can be greatly alleviated or entirely relieved by hormone replacement. Life stresses can also precipitate or exacerbate menopausal symptoms, and psychological counseling which accompanies estrogen therapy can be helpful under these circumstances. Even left untreated, menopausal symptoms generally subside spontaneously in time.

During or, more usually, following menopause, large numbers of older women begin to show signs of estrogen or sex-steroid deprivation, which can affect their sexual functioning. Many women complain of a feeling of "dryness" or "loss of juices" in the vagina, particularly during sexual intercourse. Vaginal lubrication produced by congestion of the blood vessels in the vaginal wall is the physiological equivalent of erection in the man. Lubrication of the walls of the vagina begins to take longer as a woman grows older. This seems to be due both to the loss of estrogen necessary for its production and to changes in the structure of the vaginal wall itself through which the secretions ooze. When this happens, intercourse may feel scratchy, rough and eventually painful.

Typically, the lining of the vagina begins to thin and become easily irritated, leading to pain and perhaps cracking and bleeding during and after intercourse. The vagina can no longer as easily absorb the shock of a thrusting penis. Such pain (dyspareunia) occurs especially if intercourse is of long duration or following a long period without sexual contact. Sometimes the shape of the vagina itself changes, becoming narrower, shorter and less elastic, although it generally continues to be more than large enough for intercourse. The usual remedy is estrogen replacement by mouth or by vaginal application. In extreme cases, the physician will very occasionally resort to **artificial dilation (enlargement) of the vagina or to surgery.**

With loss of estrogen, the usually acid vaginal secretions become less acidic, increasing the possibility of vaginal infection, and causing burning, itching, and discharge. This condition is variously called estrogen-deficient, steroid-deficient, atrophic or "senile" vaginitis.* If infection spreads to the bladder, it produces an inflammation called cystitis if it is not treated. These conditions are curable, but they should be treated by a doctor. Home douching should not be attempted unless your doctor instructs you to do so,

---

* It should not be assumed that all vaginal itching and discharge is "senile vaginitis." There should be a complete examination, including the Pap test, to rule out the possibility of a tumor of the reproductive tract. Allergies, trichomonas, fungus infections (especially in diabetics) and worries are other causes of itching; womb prolapse (fallen womb) may produce a discharge.

because it can confuse the diagnosis and may not, in any case, be the recommended treatment.

With the thinning of the vaginal walls, the bladder and urethra (the tube through which the urine is passed) are less protected and may be irritated during intercourse. Older women can develop what is sometimes called "honeymoon cystitis," an inflammation of the bladder resulting from bruising and jostling. This tends to be an irritative condition initially, rather than a bacterial infection. When bacteria are present, however, it becomes a full-fledged cystitis, characterized by an unrelenting, irresistible urge to urinate, accompanied by a burning sensation, and must be treated medically. Advanced stages bring an increasingly painful burning during urination, waking at night to urinate and, occasionally, blood in the urine.

The clitoris may be slightly reduced in size very late in life, although this is not always the case. The lips of the vagina (the labia) may become less firm. The covering of the clitoris and the fat pad in the hair-covered pubic area lose some of their fatty tissue, leaving the clitoris less protected and more easily irritated. However, it still remains the source of intense sexual sensation and orgasm, essentially as it was in earlier years.

Women in good health who were able to have orgasms in their younger years can continue having orgasms until very late in life, well into the eighties. (Indeed, some women begin to have orgasms for the first time as they grow older. Lack of orgasmic ability earlier in life does not necessarily mean that such a pattern will continue.) Shorter-lasting orgasms and spasms in the uterus, when they occur, are evidence of hormonal insufficiency and can be treated. Some women undergo a marked decrease in general well-being, with a resultant weakening of sexual interest that is related to estrogen deprivation. This may be alleviated or completely eliminated with treatment. However, additional estrogens do not directly stimulate sexual arousal in women. Interestingly, male hormones do, but they are not useful in treating women because of their potential masculinizing effects.

TREATMENT OF POSTMENOPAUSAL CHANGES

Regular Sexual Activity. Women who have had patterns of regular sexual intercourse once or twice a week over the years seem to experience fewer symptoms of sexual dysfunction than women with patterns of irregular and infrequent intercourse. Even though older women with regular patterns may show physical signs of steroid insufficiency, their lubricating capacity continues unimpaired, while regular contractions during intercourse and orgasm maintain vaginal muscle tone. Contact with a penis also helps preserve the shape and size of the vaginal space.

It is, of course, impossible for numbers of older women to continue sexual contact after the illness or death of their partners. Many other women have never married or are divorced or separated. For them, self-stimulation (masturbation) can be effective in preserving lubricating ability and the muscle tone which maintains the size and shape of the vagina. In addition, it can release tensions, stimulate sexual appetite and contribute to general well-being. We fully realize that many older women are not prepared to view masturbation in a positive light. We shall discuss this important subject further in Chapter 6.

Hormone Replacement Therapy. When sex hormones diminish during menopause, sex-steroid therapy to replace them can reduce many symptoms substantially, including the physiological responses to the menopause process itself and the effects of sex-steroid deprivation which appear after menopause has been completed. Thinning of the vaginal walls, loss of vaginal elasticity, vaginitis and dryness all respond well to local applications of vaginal estrogen creams and suppositories. The natural estrogen complex, usually taken internally in the form of a pill, can be effective in reducing and reversing many symptoms. All estrogen therapy *must* be prescribed and regulated by a doctor. Although estrogens are widely and helpfully used, they are complex substances and not for self-administration.

The natural estrogen complex has been in use for thirty or more years. It is relatively inexpensive and effective. The dosage for menopausal and postmenopausal estrogen deficiency, including atrophic vaginitis and pruritus vulvae, may be determined, in part, by the Maturation Index laboratory test of vaginal cells, performed by a physician. Estrogen is usually taken for three weeks, followed by one week off; the correct dosage to be determined by the physician. Synthetic estrogens are generally cheaper and more powerful than natural forms, but they do tend to have more uncomfortable and sometimes serious side effects.

Sensitiveness to estrogens varies greatly from woman to woman. Too much estrogen can cause fluid retention and weight gain, gastrointestinal disturbances, breast and pelvic pain from swollen tissues, headaches, high blood pressure, vaginal discharge and skin pigmentation, any of which should be evaluated by a doctor if it occurs. Any vaginal bleeding should also be checked.

Few physicians feel that *all* women

should receive estrogen therapy, and most administer it only to those experiencing serious discomfort. Physicians vary in their opinions as to when women should begin taking estrogens internally: during menopause, after it has ended, or only when steroid-deficiency symptoms appear.

In view of recent evidence concerning the possible relationship of estrogen to an increased incidence of uterine cancer in some women, it is imperative that physicians and their patients evaluate the wisdom of using estrogens, the dosage levels, and the length of time treatment is to be given. The Federal Government's Food and Drug Administration has recommended that estrogen be administered at the lowest effective dose for the shortest possible time. Further scientific studies will be necessary to evaluate the amount of risk that may be present and to weigh this against possible benefits.

Aside from distinct menopausal symptoms, another factor involved in deciding if and when a woman should take estrogens is the appearance of certain physical conditions: arteriosclerosis (hardening of the arteries), osteoporosis (leading to chronic backache, compression fractures of the back and "dowager's hump"), atrophy of fatty tissues and loss of skin elasticity, which may follow the menopause. Estrogen may be helpful in preventing or treating these conditions.

While the exact role of estrogens in uterine cancer is being clarified by further studies, it is also important to know that estrogens *may* delay the diagnosis of cancer if patient and doctor attribute vaginal bleeding to the withdrawal of estrogen and do not consider other possible causes. Any woman in whom menses have ceased who starts bleeding (whether during the weeks she is taking estrogen *or* the week off) should see her doctor at once and have a Pap smear or other diagnostic tests.

Estrogens may also affect the spread of *already existing* cancer of the reproductive system and the breasts; therefore they should be given internally only after careful medical examination, followed by twice-yearly Pap smears and vaginal and breast examinations. Women should learn to give themselves monthly breast examinations. Many gynecologists believe estrogen therapy should not be given to women with recurrent chronic mastitis (tendency to cyst formation) or abnormal mamograms (special X-rays of the breasts); others disagree. Estrogens may increase the risk of gall bladder trouble. Severe kidney or liver disease, some heart problems, overweight, high blood pressure and diabetes, or a personal or family history of breast or uterine cancer may be contraindications for estrogen.

Some women have few or no symptoms that impair their sexual functioning, even if they are not treated with sex steroids. Such women apparently continue to produce sex steroids on their own after menopause, although in reduced quantities, because these steroids originate not only in the ovaries but also in the adrenal glands. In addition, as mentioned earlier, women with opportunity for regular sexual activity show fewer problems. There is some indication that regular sexual activity actually stimulates estrogen production.

Home Remedies. If women are experiencing minimal discomfort and do not wish to use estrogen, a simple lubricant that dissolves in water (for example, K-Y jelly) can be placed in the vagina before intercourse to reduce dryness and friction. Do *not* use petroleum jelly (Vaseline) because it does not dissolve in water and can be a vehicle for vaginal infection.

The discomfort of "honeymoon cystitis" may be alleviated by changes in sexual positioning. The male partner should thrust his penis downward toward the back of the vagina and in the direction of the rectum, rather than toward the upper part of the vagina. This protects the bladder and delicate urethra.

Bacterial or viral cystitis is often preventable or reversible. If there is a predisposition to infection, careful washing of the woman's vaginal area and the man's penis with soap and water before sexual activity helps reduce the possibility. Older women should urinate before love-making since a full bladder is more easily irritated. Immediately after intercourse it is helpful to drink large amounts of water and urinate frequently to flush out any disease agents. If symptoms persist, medical care is necessary.

If home douching is recommended by a physician for a vaginal infection, an ordinary cleansing douche is two tablespoons of white vinegar mixed with two quarts of quite warm — not hot — water. Fill a clean douche bag (or a hot-water bottle with a douching attachment) with the fluid, hang the container a foot or so above the floor of the bathtub and lie down in the tub. Insert the nozzle about an inch and a half into the vagina and *slowly* release the clamp so the water runs in gently and drains back out. Baking soda (one tablespoon per quart of water) is sometimes recommended instead of vinegar; follow the doctor's recommendation.

As a preventive measure, the wearing of cotton panties rather than nonabsorbent nylon or other synthetics can help avoid infections by allowing air to circulate in the vaginal area. For the same reason, snug girdles, pantyhose and tight slacks should not be worn by women susceptible to infection.

Since the clitoral area of older women is often more sensitive to trauma or irritation, sexual partners need to be thoughtful about touching this area in a way that does not produce pain. Older women should be frank in telling their partners what is pleasurable and what is not.

OLDER MEN

Most men begin to worry secretly about sexual aging some time in their thirties, when they compare their present level of sexual activity with their previous performance as teen-agers and very young adults. These worries tend to accelerate in the forties and fifties and reach a peak in the sixties as definite sexual changes continue to be observed.

What changes do men notice? Quite simply, their penises don't work in the same way as they did at a younger age. Lacking understanding of these changes, men misinterpret them as alarming evidence of either the onset of impotence or its future inevitability. "From a psychosexual point of view," say Masters and Johnson, "the male over age 50 has to contend with one of the great fallacies of our culture. Every man in this age group is arbitrarily identified by both public and professional alike as sexually impaired."

Potency is the man's sexual capacity for intercourse. Impotence is the temporary or permanent incapacity to have an erection sufficient to carry out the sexual act. (Sterility should not be confused with impotence. It refers to infertility or the incapacity to father children.) What is normal potency for one man may not be normal for another. There are variations in the frequency of erection and the length of time an erection is maintained. Such individual differences often continue over many years, defining unique personal patterns. Therefore comparisons of a man's present sexual status must be made in terms of his past and present history and not against some generalized "standard."

Allowing for individual variations from

man to man, a number of gradual and fairly predictable processes are associated with chronological aging. The older man ordinarily takes longer to obtain an erection than a younger man. The difference is a matter of minutes after sexual stimulation rather than a few seconds. The erection may also not be quite as large, straight and hard as in previous years. Once the man is fully excited, however, his erection will usually be sturdy and reliable, particularly if this was the pattern in earlier life.

Premature ejaculation, which is psychologically induced, does not tend to develop for the first time in the later years. It is a symptom that evolves in the earlier years but may continue into later life. Fortunately it is subject to treatment, for instance by the "squeeze" technique, in which the sexual partner presses the penis in such a manner as to stop ejaculation. The partner grasps the end of the erect penis with the thumb and first two fingers (where the shaft meets the glans) and squeezes strongly for several seconds. This causes the man to lose his urge to ejaculate but allows the couple to continue love-making. By alternating the squeezing with sex play, a couple may delay ejaculation until they are ready for a climax. In addition, premature ejaculation may become less of a problem as a man grows older simply because some of the urgency to ejaculate diminishes.

The lubrication that appears prior to ejaculation (Cowper's gland secretory activity) becomes reduced or disappears completely as men age, but this has little effect on sexual performance. There is also a reduction in the volume of seminal fluid, and this results in a decrease in the need to ejaculate. Younger men produce three to five ml. of semen (about one teaspoon) every twenty-four hours, while men past fifty produce two to three ml. Actually this can be a decided advantage in love-making since it means that the older man can delay ejaculation more easily and thus make love longer, extending his own enjoyment and enhancing the possibility of orgasm for his partner.

Orgasms may begin to feel different with age. The younger man is aware of a few pleasurable seconds, just before ejaculation, when he can no longer control himself. As ejaculation occurs, powerful contractions are felt and the semen spurts with a force which can carry it one to two feet from the tip of the penis. With an older man there may be a briefer period of awareness before ejaculation or no such period at all. (In some men, however, this period actually lengthens because of spasm in the prostate.) The orgasm itself is generally less explosive, in that semen is propelled a shorter distance and contractions are less forceful. *None* of these physiological changes interfere with the aging man's experiencing extreme orgasmic pleasure, even when the pre-ejaculation stage is altered or completely missing.

The forcefulness of orgasm also lessens naturally when a couple voluntarily prolong their love-making before orgasm. Older men have a choice of an extended period of sexual pleasure with a milder orgasm or a briefer session with a more intense orgasm.

Whereas younger men can usually have

another erection in a matter of minutes after orgasm, the older man must wait a longer period of time (the refractory period), from many hours up to several days, before a full erection is again possible. In addition, in contrast to a younger man's pattern of minutes or even hours in losing his erection, the older man rapidly loses his following orgasm, often so quickly that the penis literally slips out of the vagina. This is not a sign of impairment of the penis and its erectile capacity.

Older men need not fall into the common trap of measuring manhood by the frequency with which they can carry intercourse through to ejaculation. Some men over sixty are physically satisfied with one or two ejaculations per week because of the decrease of semen production. Others, particularly if they were sexually less active earlier in life, do not ejaculate this frequently. Whatever the customary frequency, and although they can often force themselves to ejaculate more often, if left to choice each man finds his own level. Remember that love-making need not be limited to ejaculatory ability. Men who are knowledgeable and comfortable about themselves may have intercourse as frequently as they wish but ejaculate perhaps only once out of every two or three times that they make love. By delaying ejaculation, the older man can rapidly become erect over and over again, continuing with intercourse and the pleasurable feelings it arouses as often and as long as he and his partner wish. It is therefore useful for men and women to question the notion that an ejaculation is obligatory with each sexual contact, and each man should find his own schedule for ejaculation.

Male fertility — sperm production — generally ends in the mid-seventies, though there have been instances where it continued into the nineties. A urologist can test for the presence of live sperm through microscopic examination of semen. It is important to repeat that fertility has no connection with potency; even if a man loses his capacity to father children, his ability to have intercourse is not affected.

In general, men do not lose their

capacity to have erections and ejaculations as they age. Problems which may occur, particularly impotence, are usually caused by physical or psychological difficulties and are generally treatable. In addition, a pattern of regular sexual activity helps preserve sexual functioning.

Is There a Male Menopause? Do men experience a period in life which is physically or psychologically comparable to the female cessation of menstruation and loss of estrogen hormones? There is certainly no physical "menopause" or climacteric in men analogous to that in women, because hormone loss in men does not occur precipitously.* Decreases in the male hormone testosterone take place very gradually as one grows older, and there are wide variations from man to man. In fact, the rate of decline slows later in life. Some older men actually have testosterone levels identical with those in young men. Few men have specific physiological

---

*Actually, hormone loss in women occurs *in spurts,* and never in a single abrupt cessation.

symptoms which can be traced directly to lowered androgen levels. Distinct psychological symptoms are also rare and can usually be accounted for by other circumstances in a man's life, such as his reactions to retirement, to aging in general or to other stresses.

As research on male hormone levels becomes more sophisticated and reliable, it may eventually be possible to define a male climacteric, particularly with reference to some of the sexual changes which now accompany male aging. However, it will be quite different from our concept of female menopause, with far less distinct and less predictable symptoms.

ARE WE TALKING ABOUT "AGING" OR DISEASE PROCESSES?

We do not yet know whether all the physiological changes we have described in this chapter, especially in men, are "normal aging" processes or symptoms of reversible physical conditions. Certainly, replacement hormones have already done much for women. The same may eventually be true for men. The fact that a man takes longer to achieve an erection as he gets older, or requires a longer period of time before an erection can occur again after the last sexual act, may possibly be related to reduced nutritive, oxygen and blood supplies because of hardening of the arteries (what doctors call arteriosclerosis). From a variety of recent studies we already know that much physical change that has been attributed to aging is, in fact, due to a variety of other factors, notably the vascular diseases. The integrative systems of the body that link so many of its functions — the circulatory system, the endocrine or hormonal system, the central nervous system — all play a role in the decline of functioning when they are affected by diseases. We are only beginning to have some knowledge of the fundamentals of the aging process itself: whether there is a central-nervous-system pacemaker that dictates changes; whether there are reductions in the speed of reactions and in metabolism.

It is possible that in the future we will find sexual activity among older people actually improving as we increasingly separate out the diseases of old age from aging processes, and begin to prevent and treat these diseases on a wide scale. Furthermore, if aging factors become more clear-cut and if agents directly retarding the process of aging are found, there will be still further changes in the sexual picture. What relatively healthy men and women need to remember, even under the limitations of our present knowledge about aging, is that sexual activity — to whatever degree and in whatever forms they want to express it — should continue to be possible, normal, pleasurable and beneficial.* Those older people with fairly common chronic ailments can also adapt their sexual desires to satisfactory expression in many cases. Neither age nor most infirmity automatically spells the end of sex.

*For further detail on physical aging and sex, see the pioneering clinical chapters on the aging male and female in *Human Sexual Inadequacy* by William H. Masters and Virginia E. Johnson, Boston: Little, Brown & Co., 1970, pp. 316 - 350.

3

Common Medical Problems and Sex

ILLNESS AND SEX

Obviously, illness affects people sexually. An acute illness which is sudden and severe has an immediate effect. The body becomes totally involved in meeting the physical threat, and anxiety is strong until the crisis has passed and the full extent of the illness is known. Understandably, people in these circumstances have little or no energy and attention left for sexual feelings. Once the acute phase is over, most people return slowly to sexuality; but if recovery time is lengthy or if the illness results in a chronic condition which must be lived with, there can be problems. We will discuss several of the more common conditions which may directly affect sexuality in persons over sixty.

Heart Disease. In the forty-five-to-sixty-four-year age group the occurrence of heart disease is nearly three times as great in men as in women. After sixty-five the rates become more equalized, and it is believed the postmenopausal woman is less protected because of reduction in estrogen levels.

Heart attacks (coronary attacks) lead many people to give up sex altogether under the assumption that it will endanger their lives. Most physicians do recommend that sexual intercourse be discontinued for a period of weeks or months (roughly eight to fourteen weeks — check with your doctor) immediately following an attack, to give healing processes plenty of time.* But after that, many experts feel, sex can and should be resumed, depending on the

*Masturbation can begin long before you are ready for sexual intercourse and is a good way to begin to get back into action.

patient's interest, general fitness and conditioning. Some propose a functional test to determine when it is safe to resume: If you can walk briskly for three blocks without distress in the chest, pain, palpitations or shortness of breath, you are usually well enough for sex.

Sex can be carried out safely without sacrificing pleasure and quality. Studies tell us that, on the average, couples take ten to sixteen minutes for the sex act. The oxygen usage (or "cost") in sex approximates climbing one or two flights of stairs, walking rapidly at a rate of two to two and a half miles per hour, or completing many common occupational tasks. In average sexual activity the heart rate ranges from 90 to 160 beats per minute, which is the level for light to moderate physical activity. Systolic blood pressure (the upper reading, which reflects the contraction phase of the heart's action) may double from 120 to over 240, and the respiratory rate rises from 16 or 18 to about 60 breaths per minute. These "vital signs" increase only slightly more in men than in women, perhaps due in part to the usual sexual position of the man on top. Intercourse conducted side-by-side or with the woman on top can help to reduce the exertion of the man if he is the one with the heart problem. These positions avoid sapping of energy from prolonged use of the arms and legs to support the body. Proper physical conditioning under the doctor's guidance can also be useful.

Physical-fitness programs enhance heart performance for a variety of activities, including sex.* Before undertaking an exercise program you can ask your doctor to arrange special testing in which an electrocardiogram (EKG, recorded by an instrument that traces the heart's electric currents and provides information regarding the heart's actions in health and disease) is taken while you are conducted through various levels of exercise. This is a "Stress EKG." An electromagnetic tape recording of your EKG during the sexual

*Isometric exercises may be unwise for certain kinds of patients because they cause pressure changes in the aorta, the major blood vessel from the heart. Check with your physician.

act can even be made in your own home. This is called Hellerstein's Sexercise Tolerance Test. Drs. H. E. Hellerstein and E. H. Friedman studied the sexual activity of men after recovery from an acute heart attack by monitoring sexual activities in the privacy of their patients' homes. They reported that if the patient could perform exercise at levels of vigorous walking and other special activities without symptoms of abnormal pulse rate, blood pressure or EKG changes, it was generally safe to recommend the resumption of sexual activity and most types of industrial employment.

It must be remembered that physical exercise leads to less likelihood of a heart attack. The sedentary person may be more prone to coronary attacks and less apt to survive the experience if one occurs. Too much food and drink before sexual intercourse can also place a strain on the heart. Of course, if the condition of the heart has deteriorated to the point that attack is imminent, it will occur with any physical exertion, not merely sex. It should also be realized that sexual arousal alone (without intercourse) affects the vital signs — although not as intensely as the sexual act itself. Thus failure to provide sexual release may prolong arousal, causing psychological frustration that will probably produce some adverse physical effects. Finally, many everyday nonsexual activities that people are not likely to give up produce more increased heart and respiratory rates than sexual intercourse.

Impotence can follow a heart attack for both physical and psychological reasons. A man may experience chest pain (angina pectoris) during various forms of exertion, including sex, that frightens him and prevents erection. To counteract this pain, coronary dilators such as nitroglycerin, prescribed by a physician, can be taken to improve circulation and reduce pain just prior to intercourse. A second common and understandable cause of impotence is fear of inducing another coronary and risking death. Yet the incidence of death during intercourse is estimated at less than one percent of sudden coronary deaths. (In one major study the rate was less than 0.3 percent!) Of this small percentage, seven out of ten deaths occur in extramarital relations, suggesting that the stressful aspects associated with such affairs, such as hurry, guilt and anxiety, are a factor.

Physicians do not always advise their patients adequately on the resumption of sexual activity after a heart attack. They may be too conservative or fail to realize the importance of sex to the patient. If you want to know more than your doctor has told you, it may be necessary to ask for specific information and directions, including a program of physical conditioning. Your sexual partner also needs to be fully informed and counseled about any changes in life style, including lovemaking, that may be necessary. *Under most circumstances there is little reason to abstain from sex after a heart attack and many reasons to continue.* Pleasure, exhilaration, release of tension, mild exercise, and a sense of well-being are some of the benefits.

Episodes of congestive heart failure are also commonly called heart attacks. When compensated by digitalis, diuretics and diet, sex is again an active possibility. Two to three weeks for recovery is advised before resuming sex. You should be able to walk briskly for three blocks without shortness of breath.

Patients with cardiac pacemakers need not give up sex. Limitations on all forms of physical activity are advised during the first two weeks following implantation to allow healing. Otherwise the guideline to follow is an evaluation of the underlying cardiac condition.

It is safe for most patients with heart disease due to hypertension — high blood pressure — to have sex. (Many people with hypertension have no significant impairment of heart function.) Patients with average to moderate hypertension, men or women, need not restrict themselves sexually. They should, however, have their hypertension well controlled by drug therapy and maintain good physical fitness. Very severe cases of hypertension may require some modification of sexual activity; your doctor is the best judge of this.

Strokes. Strokes (cerebrovascular accidents) do not necessitate the discontinuance of sexual activity. It is extremely unlikely that further strokes can be produced through sexual exertion. If paralysis has occurred, appropriate sexual positions chosen to compensate for it can be used.

Diabetes. Sugar diabetes (diabetes mellitus) is common in late life. Most men with diabetes are *not* impotent, but it is one of the few illnesses which can directly cause chronic impotence in men. Impotence occurs two to five times as often in diabetics as in the general population, even though sexual interest and desire may continue. Indeed, impotence is often the first symptom of diabetes. Most cases of diabetic-produced impotence are reversible. If the disease has been poorly controlled, there is a fair chance that proper regulation thereafter will improve potency. When impotence occurs in well-controlled diabetes, it may be permanent. (Unfortunately, if you have been diabetic for a long time, the chances are greater that the impotence will be chronic and irreversible.) It is more difficult to evaluate the effects of diabetes on the sexuality of women since they do not have an obvious physical indicator like erection.

Arthritis. There are two major forms of arthritis that may cause pain during sexual activity. In rheumatoid arthritis, medications such as simple aspirin to reduce this pain and experimentation with new sexual positions which do not aggravate pain in sensitive joints are often helpful. A well-established program of exercise, rest and warm baths is especially useful in reducing arthritic discomfort and in facilitating sex.* Indeed, much of the crippling by rheumatoid arthritis results from inactivity. A person tends to keep his

*See the excellent *Home Care Programs in Arthritis: A Manual for Patients,* published by the Arthritis Foundation, 1969, and available free, 1212 Avenue of the Americas, New York, N.Y. 10036. The exercises described in this booklet are basic but should be cleared with your own doctor. You should do them regularly, and not stop them when you are feeling either "good" or "bad." We also recommend the paperback book, *The Arthritic Handbook* by Darrell C. Crain, M.D., Arco Publishing Company, 219 Park Avenue South, New York, N.Y. 10003.

painful joints in comfortable positions, and they become stiffened, even "frozen."

Exercises can be prescribed by your doctor and should include a full range of motions for your joints, strengthening and stretching of muscles, as well as encouragement of the usual and necessary household and outside activities. Maintain an erect position when standing and walking. Sit upright in a straight-back chair. Rest in bed for short periods several times during the day. In general, you should rest or sleep in a straight position, flat on your back. You can use a small pillow under your head but *not* under your knees, for this can lead to stiff, bent knees.

Heat relaxes muscle spasm and is useful before undertaking your exercise program and also prior to sex. Various types of heat can be used, such as heat lamps, heating pads, warm compresses, tub baths, showers and paraffin baths. A daily tub with warm but not hot water and for no more than twenty minutes is excellent. If you stay in the bath too long, it can be fatiguing. During intercourse the side-by-side position may be preferred by both men and women, especially when the patient has many tender areas and pain trigger points. Experiment until you find positions that work best for you.

There is evidence suggesting that regular sex activity helps rheumatoid arthritis, probably because of adrenal gland production of the hormone cortisone, and because of the physical activity involved. In addition, emotional stress can result from sexual dissatisfaction, and since stress worsens arthritis, sexual activity can be helpful in maintaining good functioning.

Osteoarthritis (the "wear-and-tear" disease of the joints that comes with advancing years) is usually mild and not inflammatory. This arthritis rarely interferes with sex.

Anemia. One out of four people over sixty has some measure of anemia, a common cause of fatigue and consequent reduction of sexual activity. Anemia may develop insidiously following even a mild general or localized infection, or as the result of a poor diet. Tiredness, loss of appetite and headaches are some of its early symptoms. Since anemia is the symptom of a number of diseases, comprehensive medical examination is indicated. Follow-up treatment is important. Often an improved diet with adequate vitamins and minerals is all that is necessary to restore both energy and sexual activity.

Backache. Backache in the small of the back near the base of the spine is common among older people. Perhaps the most frequent cause is strain produced by sudden use of back muscles in a generally inactive person. In women it can be caused by osteoporosis (postmenopausal softening of the bones), related to reduction of estrogen levels. Slipped discs and arthritis are other causes of backache in both men and women.

A firm mattress and bed board are needed by most backache sufferers. A plywood board at least one-half inch thick and the same size as the mattress can be placed between the mattress and springs for extra support. Exercise is helpful for most forms of backache, but you should see your doctor for instructions in your particular case. Women with osteoporosis may receive relief from estrogens as well as exercise. Slipped discs often respond well to exercise but sometimes may require prolonged bed rest; otherwise surgery may be necessary. Sufferers from arthritic backache should follow the program described above for arthritis. Sexual activity itself is an excellent form of exercise therapy for the back, stomach and pelvic muscles, and if undertaken in a regular and reasonably vigorous manner can help reduce back pain. During sex, the side position may be most comfortable if back muscles are tender. Or the backache sufferer may prefer lying on his or her back, with the partner on top. Areas of discomfort can be supported by pillows.

Hernia or Rupture. A hernia or rupture is the protrusion of a part of the intestine through a gap or weak point in the muscular abdominal wall that contains it. The main complication to avoid is strangulation, the cutting off of the blood supply with resulting death of tissue, which is a true surgical emergency. Straining of any kind, including straining during sexual intercourse, can sometimes increase hernia symptoms such as pain and, rarely, induce strangulation. Many surgeons recommend corrective surgery early rather than waiting for an emergency to arise.

Parkinson's Disease. Parkinson's disease is a progressive nervous-system disorder of the later years marked by tremor, slowness of movement, partial facial paralysis and peculiarity of posture and gait. Depression is commonly associated with Parkinson's disease and may lead to impotence in men and lack of sexual interest in both sexes. When there is advanced organic involvement, however, impotence may be physically connected with the disease. Patients with Parkinson's disease who are treated with drugs such as L-dopa may show improved sexual performance, largely because of their generally increased sense of well-being and greater mobility.

Chronic Prostatitis. Diminished sexual desire in men may be associated with chronic prostatitis. This disease is an inflammation of the prostate gland, a walnut-sized organ located just beneath the bladder in the male. It produces the milky lubricating fluid which transports sperm during sexual intercourse. Prostatitis is characterized by a history of cloudy white discharge from the penis, usually in the morning or while straining on the toilet. Pain in the perineal region (the area between the scrotum and the anus) and in the end of the penis on urination and ejaculation may be present. Massage of the prostate causes tenderness. Treatment includes antibiotics, warm sitz baths and periodic gentle prostatic massage by a physician. Sexual desire usually returns after pain lessens, especially when the pain after ejaculation is eliminated.

Many doctors believe prostatitis can be caused by both too frequent and too infrequent sex. The basis for some pain between the anus and the scrotum after ejaculation may be mild prostatitis; other causes are congestion due to excessive or lengthy preliminary sexual arousal, or an unsatisfying orgasm. However, a more common cause is infrequent sex, which results in congestion in the pelvic area. Treatment in these cases consists of more frequent sexual intercourse as well as prostatic massage and warm sitz baths.

Whenever chronic prostatitis is a possibility, one should avoid excessive alcohol. Should urinary retention develop following sexual intercourse, as it occasionally does, it may be caused by the combination of a large fluid intake and the sedative effect of alcohol. If there is also some enlargement of the prostate without inflammation, excessive fluid intake, including alcohol, may lead to retention of urine.

Stress Incontinence. Some women develop stress incontinence (caused by prolapse of the bladder), a condition in which there is a seepage of urine because of a momentary inability to control their bladder. This happens particularly when they laugh, cough, engage in sex or otherwise exert themselves. Dyspareunia, or painful intercourse, may also be present. Stress incontinence is most frequently seen in women who have had a number of children, sometimes with unrepaired injuries following childbirth, with resulting relaxation of the supports of the uterus and bladder. It is also seen in women who have had their uterus removed surgically (hysterectomy). Slack supporting tissues may cause the bladder to protrude into the vagina (cystocele). Estrogen, taken by mouth or applied locally in the form of cream, may help firm up the vaginal lining and thus reduce the irritation from the protruding bladder. Special exercises, called Kegel's exercises (described on page 120), are very useful. In severe cases, surgery may be required to tighten the supporting tissues.

Herniation, or prolapse of the uterus and of the rectum (rectocele), may occur alone or in association with prolapse of the bladder. Surgical treatment is usually effective.

Excessively Enlarged Vagina. Women who have had a number of children, or difficult childbirths, or tears in the opening of the vagina at the time of childbirth may have an excessively enlarged vagina. An anterior and posterior plastic repair, a surgical procedure, may reconstruct the vagina effectively and make sex more pleasurable.

Peyronie's Disease. This disease, found in men, produces an upward bowing of the penis with the shaft angled to the right or left. A fibrous thickening of the walls of the blood vessels (*corpora cavernosa*) of the penis produces the symptoms, but its cause is unknown. Results of treatment are not predictable. Symptoms sometimes disappear spontaneously after four years or so. Current therapy is p-aminobenzoate (in the form of Potaba or Potaba Plus) for about six months. Cortisone taken orally or by injection is sometimes effective. There is no evidence that Vitamin E works. Intercourse can be painful and, if the penis is angled too far, impossible. However, in most cases of Peyronie's disease sex can continue. This ailment is thought to be rare, but we have seen enough of it to suspect it may be more common than is believed.

If you have had to abstain from sex for a medical reason for any length of time, some readjustment will be necessary when sexual activity is resumed. Irregular or infrequent sexual stimulation can interfere with healthy sexual functioning, adversely affecting potency in men and lubrication, vaginal shape and muscle tone in women. These difficulties are likely to taper off as activity is resumed and one should not be discouraged by initial difficulties. When a sexual partner is not available (as, for example, in widowhood) or circumstances do not permit contact with a partner, both men and women can protect much of their sexual capacity through regular masturbation, unless this is personally unacceptable.

IMPOTENCE BASED
ON PHYSICAL CAUSES

Impotence is the loss of a man's ability to obtain an erection sufficient for sexual intercourse. It is *not* part of the normal aging process. Since older men are capable of performing sexually, if impotence occurs, it is important to investigate the cause or causes and to treat the condition. *Most* impotence is psychologically based, and this will be discussed in Chapter 4; but it can sometimes be produced by or associated with organic diseases. Therefore it is imperative for a man to be examined medically to determine whether or not a physical condition is acting as a partial, or complete, cause of his impotence. The following man's situation is illustrative:

I am going to be 76 years old and just married a 60-year-old woman last year. We had a perfect relationship for three months. Then I had a bout of flu and lost my strength. Now I am getting my strength back and I have no feeling and no erection. My wife is discouraged, and my doctor just tells me to take vitamins.

This man has "secondary impotence," which means that he was potent for at least part of his life but that at some point potency became a problem.* The severity of impotence ranges from being incapable of erection some of the time to incapacity most of or all of the time. Impotence also refers to the inability to *sustain* an erection for long even if one can get one. Lack of a morning erection upon awakening is strongly diagnostic of a physical basis for the problem. (On the other hand, nocturnal erections and emissions ["wet dreams"] and the ability to achieve an erection on masturbation or on awakening are favorable signs of continued physical potency and point to a psychological basis for any problems.)

There are a number of physical causes of secondary sexual impotence. Impotence

*"Primary impotence" is a relatively rare condition in which a man has never been able to have an erection sufficient for sexual intercourse.

due to the more common causes is often reversible. Drugs — particularly antihypertensive medications, tranquilizers and antidepressants — are very often responsible. When these are discontinued, potency typically returns. Alcohol is a major culprit; though it may enhance desire, it often damages the capacity for sexual activity.

Diabetes (as mentioned earlier) and some rarer hormonal diseases can cause impotence which is often reversible. As we shall see later, one of the three common procedures used to surgically reduce the size of the prostate may sometimes produce impotence. There can be neurological (nervous system) bases for impotence. Impairment of blood circulation is a frequent cause, and it, too, is often responsive to treatment. In one condition, the Leriche syndrome, there is an intermittent reduction of the blood supply needed for erection. Discomfort in the thighs or limping, which is relieved by rest, often accompanies this syndrome. Surgical correction can restore sexual potency and eliminate the limp.

Medical treatment for secondary impotence includes treatment of specific underlying diseases and, occasionally, successful treatment with hormones. At present, male hormone therapy (sex-steroid replacement) is controversial and experimental. Replacement of the male hormone testosterone has little known permanent beneficial effect on the sexual problems of older men, particularly impotence, unless there is definitely proven testicular deficiency in the production of male hormones (hypogonadism, a rare condition). Any benefit from testosterone should show up in three to four weeks, but even in those men who do appear to respond to such treatment, improvement is generally short-lived.* Beneficial effects do not tend to be maintained indefinitely despite continued hormone administration

*There are physicians, among them endocrinologist Dr. Robert Greenblatt, who are more sanguine about the effectiveness and safety of testosterone therapy for impotence, particularly when the hormone is administered intramuscularly (by injection) in a specified regimen. The individual's doctor must determine this.

except in clear-cut deficiencies. There may be side effects such as fluid retention, and evidence indicates that testosterone may stimulate already existing prostatic growth; thus it should not be given if the prostate gland is enlarged.

A penile prosthesis (rigid implant of silicone or a splint) may be used in intransigent organic impotence with occasional success. A so-called rubber doughnut may also help. (It is of no use in absolute impotence.) This hard rubber device is slipped over the partially erect penis. It fits tightly at the base and retains the blood in the penis necessary for erection.

Because impotence is such a widespread concern, a host of questionable treatments has evolved. Folklore is full of reputed "remedies." Doctors have been known to prescribe oysters, greens and massive amounts of Vitamins B_{12} and E. There are also "youth doctors" and nonmedical entrepreneurs who produce and sell countless substances and gadgets advertised to rejuvenate sexual potency. Older people are particular targets of fraudulent consumer schemes and devices that promise to "make you look younger" and "guarantee" to prevent or cure impotence. The U.S. Postal Service provided us with a representative list of worthless nostrums or alleged aphrodisiacs.* Among the popular names are "Mexican Spanish Fly in Liquid Form," "Instant Love Potion," "Sex Stimulant for Women," "Mad Dog Weed," "Magic Lure," "Super Nature Tablets," "European Love Drops" and "Linga Pendulum Penis Enlarger and Strengthener." We have tabulated by popular and scientific names a variety of alleged aphrodisiacs. Watch out for them. If they seem to work, it is only through the power of suggestion and any "cure" is likely to be temporary. Some are extremely dangerous; Spanish fly, for example, can kill.

*The Postal Service brings action against person(s) engaged in conducting a scheme or device for obtaining money or property through the mails by means of false representations in violation of Title 39, U.S. Code 30005.

Some False Aphrodisiacs

Alcohol	Especially wines
Cantharidin	Tincture of *Cantharis vesicatoria* (Spanish fly)
Capsicum	Extract of *Capsicum frutescens* (cayenne pepper from South America)
Cimicifugin	Resin from *Cimicifuga racemosa* (black snakeroot)
Cubeb	Oleoresin from *Piper cubeba* (from Java)
Damiana	From leaves of *Turnera diffusa* (from Mexico)
Ergot	Alkaloids from *Claviceps purpurea*
Marijuana	*Cannabis sativa*
Nux vomica	Extract from seeds of *Strychnos nux-vomica*
Sanguinaria	Extract from *Sanguinaria canadenis* (bloodroot)
Vitamin E	d-Alpha-tocopherol

SURGERY AND SEX

People are understandably afraid of surgery on their sex organs. They dread possible sexual consequences in addition to the usual apprehensions aroused by any surgical procedure. Women commonly believe removal of the womb (hysterectomy) or of a breast (mastectomy) makes them "less of a woman." Men worry that prostate surgery means the end of sex life altogether. It is reassuring to know that the medical evidence does not support most of these fears.

Hysterectomy (Removal of the Womb). Technically, a hysterectomy is the removal of the womb or uterus. In addition, the ovaries and Fallopian tubes may also be removed. Many hysterectomies are performed because of the presence of benign (noncancerous) tumors called fibroids, which are not troublesome so long as they remain small but may require surgery if they enlarge and produce discomfort. There is no medical evidence that careful removal of the uterus, with or without removal of the ovaries, produces *any* change in sexual desire or performance in women. Sexual problems are likely to be due to psychological fears: of sexual impairment, or loss of femininity and attractiveness to men, or loss of sexual desire. Many women worry about premature aging or are afraid they will develop masculine characteristics if they undergo a hysterectomy, but there is no basis for these worries.

There can be pain during sex (dyspareunia) if intercourse is resumed up to four weeks after hysterectomy, due to incomplete healing in the vagina. Except for this temporary discomfort, a hysterectomy has no effect on any part of the vagina involved in intercourse. Though the cervix is no longer present at the far end of the vagina, this does not affect the sexual act or desire. In women who have not yet completed the menopause and have as many children as they want, sexual desire can actually increase after surgery because pregnancy is no longer a concern. If the ovaries are removed, loss of estrogen may bring changes in the lining of the vagina, but, as we have noted, this is treatable. Those who have had monthly mood swings may find their moods stabilized. Removal of the ovaries after menopause generally produces far fewer direct symptoms than removal before menopause because the ovaries have already stopped functioning or show a substantial reduction in estrogen output. On the other hand, removal of all or parts of a woman's childbearing apparatus, powerful symbols of womanhood, often does have significant psychological effects. If the woman sees this surgery as symbolic "castration," she needs to resolve this, either on her own or with outside help. She must understand that removal does not eradicate sexuality, cause unattractiveness or diminish her womanliness.

Mastectomy (Breast Removal). While most breast lumps are found to be benign, unfortunately the likelihood of breast cancer increases with age. Breast removal, or mastectomy, is performed when a lump in the breast is found to be malignant (cancerous).* There are different kinds of mastectomies, ranging from removal of the lump and some adjacent tissue only to the removal of the entire breast, surrounding lymph glands and chest muscles. Although these operations can be lifesaving, they have understandable psychological implications for many women because they not only change the outward appearance of the body but visibly alter a specific symbol of sexuality. Breast removal can actually be more difficult to adjust to than a hysterectomy, which leaves no obvious signs beyond an abdominal scar. Although there is no physiological change in sexual capacity after mastectomy, women may temporarily lose their sexual desire out of embarrassment, their inability to accept the

---

*Early detection of breast cancer is essential to reduce unnecessary loss of life. In addition to routine examination by your physician and the use of newer techniques to help him or her in diagnosis (for example, mammography by low-voltage X-rays), you should undertake regular monthly self-examinations. See *A Breast Check* and *Facts about Breast Cancer,* available from the American Cancer Society. See also Dr. Philip Strax's *Early Detection: Breast Cancer Can Be Cured.* New York: Harper & Row, 1974, and in paperback, New American Library, 1975.

loss of the breast, and fear that they have become less attractive to their sexual partners. They are afraid the absence of the breast will be noticeable in public. A properly fitting prosthetic bra can relieve worries about public appearance, but reactions to breast loss by women themselves and their partners are not always so easily resolved. One useful technique is for women to talk frankly with other women who have already experienced a breast loss. Some physicians and hospitals arrange for such volunteers to counsel with women following surgery. The Reach to Recovery program of the American Cancer Society is a rehabilitation program for women who have had breast surgery.* It is designed to help with physical, psychological and cosmetic needs, and utilizes a carefully selected and trained corps of volunteers who have successfully adjusted to their own surgery.

Men, too, need a period of adjustment

*A helpful free booklet, *Reach to Recovery* by Terese Lasser, is available from local units of the American Cancer Society.

to work out their feelings about breast surgery in their partners. In sturdy relationships, time and affection often take care of disturbed feelings following breast removal. Severe and prolonged negative reactions may require professional psychotherapy. Do not avoid seeking aid in such cases; the odds are that it will help greatly, whether the problem is with you or your mate.

Prostatectomy (Removal of the Prostate Gland). As men get older, up to half of them will experience inflammation or enlargement of the prostate. At least half of these will require surgery. When the enlargement is noncancerous, as is usually the case, it is called benign prostatic hypertrophy (BPH).

The causes of prostatic difficulties are unknown but may be connected to changes in hormone levels. There is no foundation to the common folklore that prostate trouble is related to ''excessive'' sexual activity. Indeed, evidence suggests that an active sex life preserves healthy prostate functioning.

Since the prostate gland is so close to the bladder, its enlargement causes it to push up against the bladder or urethra, usually producing problems with urination. An enlarged prostate may increase the need to urinate or to get up to void during the night. There may be a delay in starting the stream of urine, or even a total inability to urinate. Occasionally, bleeding is present. Enlargement of the gland tends to occur slowly, and because it leads to retention and stagnation of urine there can be bacterial infection. In severe and untreated cases, damage is done to the kidneys. Surgery is absolutely necessary when a urinary shutdown occurs. Some doctors now recommend surgery at an earlier point in the course of symptoms to avoid unnecessary complications and dire emergencies; this decision is up to you and your doctor.

Three types of surgery, all requiring anesthesia, are used:

Transurethral resection, or TUR. This is the commonest and least traumatic procedure because it requires no outside incision. A thin Bakelite or plastic sheath is inserted in the penis, a tungsten wire is maneuvered through the tube, and the gland is removed. The tissue sometimes grows back following TUR. TUR is recommended chiefly when the prostate is not too enlarged, or for men after seventy.

Suprapubic (or *retropubic,* depending on whether the incision is above or behind the pubic bone). If the gland is very large, an incision is made through the abdomen to remove the tissue.

Perineal. This procedure is recommended for men with substantial prostate enlargement who, because of advanced age or physical condition, are unable to withstand the stress of prolonged anesthesia. A more radical perineal procedure is used in the surgical treatment of cancer of the gland. It can be performed with relative safety even on a very elderly man. An incision is made between the scrotum and anus (the perineum), removing most or all of the prostate.

Potency is rarely affected by the TUR and suprapubic procedures, and some men actually experience increased potency because their prostatic symptoms have been eliminated. The perineal approach — especially the radical procedure — is the chief physical cause of impotence following prostatic surgery. (Some doctors feel *only* the radical procedure may have this effect.) It also sometimes affects the ability to hold urine. For these reasons, it is generally used only when no other method is possible.

Prior to surgery prostate problems usually do not interfere with sexual functioning unless pain is present. After a prostatectomy, as we have noted, most men return to normal sexual activity. Healing time runs at least six weeks. The only change after surgery is that semen is no longer ejaculated through the opening of the penis but instead pushes backward into the bladder (retrograde ejaculation), where it is voided with the urine. This so-called dry ejaculation happens because a space has been left where the enlarged prostate had been, and fluid travels the path of least resistance to the bladder. Although men are then no longer able to father children, the large majority have erections as before, with no diminishment of sexual pleasure. In some cases even the ejaculation from the penis returns following some regrowth of the prostate;* in such instances, fertility may be restored.

By far the greatest cause of impotence occurring with prostatectomies is *psychological.* This impotence is frequently reversible. The fear is based on the tendency to associate the prostate gland with the penis since men know the two are located physically close to each other. Unfortunately, family doctors and urologists do not always give a man adequate information about what to expect after surgery, so that he falsely assumes sexual impairment.

Most prostate enlargements are noncancerous. However, all men over fifty should have a rectal examination by a physician at least once a year, and perhaps semiannually, to check the condition of the prostate. Men must also beware of the many quack remedies which usually promise treatment without surgery. Various kinds of

*A certain amount of regrowth can occur without causing difficulties before surgery is again, if ever, necessary.

massage, foods and other "cures," often at exorbitant prices, are offered to men seeking a quick remedy to a very widespread and sometimes serious condition. Avoid them and rely on your physician's advice.

Orchidectomy (Removal of the Testes). This surgery may be performed because of cancer of the prostate. The psychological impact of such castration can be devastating. Emotional preparation before surgery and counseling following surgery are indispensable. The creation of artificial testes of plastic or tantalum may also be advisable for cosmetic and emotional reasons.

Colostomy and Ileostomy (Removal of Sections of the Intestine). When part of the bowel (large intestine) must be removed for lifesaving purposes, the anus is closed and an artificial opening in the abdomen is created. The surgery may be in the colon (colostomy) or in the ileum (an ileostomy). Needless to say, the patient has many sensitive adjustments to make after such surgery. A bag is attached to the opening.

This bag fills with feces and must be emptied. There are embarrassing bowel sounds as well as odors. Much of this can be controlled adequately. Patients will have to work their way through their own feelings, however, as well as their perception of other people's attitudes. The most complicated issue of all can be the working out of the sexual relationship with one's partner. Specialized information, and perhaps counseling if it is needed, can help greatly. About a million people in the United States have had ostomies, and United Ostomy Clubs have been formed which can offer a great deal of help. There are more than 250 local chapters at present. For information on the one nearest you, contact the United Ostomy Association, Inc., 1111 Wilshire Boulevard, Los Angeles, California 90017. Patients who had active sex lives prior to ostomies usually continue to do so afterward, but inevitably there is a complex adjustment process, and you and your partner should not hesitate to seek help.

In general, for both men and women, the emotionally charged aspects of surgery which affects sex can be relatively short-lived if people spell out their fears and if their misconceptions are cleared up. Unfortunately, they often do not get the opportunity to do this. Doctors do not always take the time to explain procedures and answer questions, though counseling before surgery is extremely helpful in preventing anxiety and clarifying misunderstandings. After the operation, continued advice and emotional support from medical personnel, family and friends and special organizations are crucial to adjustment. Be sure to ask for help, and if you remain greatly troubled, seek professional psychotherapy to work through more complicated feelings.

Even under the best of modern techniques, rates of recovery vary with the individual after surgery of any kind. Some people will find their stamina or vitality reduced for some time, even though healing has been satisfactory. Surgeons do not always make it clear to their patients that these are normal variations. You have no reason to worry if this happens to you, as long as your surgeon has assured you that your postoperative recovery is progressing as it should. Once you are feeling entirely well again, your level of sexual activity will return to normal.

THE SIDE EFFECTS OF DRUGS ON SEX

Drugs — prescription and otherwise — can cause serious sexual problems for older men and women. Doctors often fail to consider this when taking medical histories from patients who report such problems and when prescribing medications. People sixty and over represent some 14 percent of the population but consume 30 percent of the drugs prescribed in this country. Tranquilizers, antidepressants and certain antihypertensive agents (for controlling high blood pressure) have all been implicated in impotence in men. Strong tranquilizers such as Mellaril (thioridazine) and other phenothiazines may cause failure to ejaculate though the capacity for erection remains intact. Any tranquilizing drug, even a mild one such as Librium (chlordiazepoxide), can also act as a depressant on the sexual feelings of women. Antidepressants such as Tofranil (imipramine hydrochloride) also inhibit the libido.

''Blocking agents'' are one class of antihypertensive drugs, including for example methyl-dopa (Aldomet), which reduces the flow of blood into the pelvic area and so inhibits erection of the penis. Another drug used against hypertension, guanethidine (Ismelin), may inhibit ejaculation by blocking the nerves involved. Reserpine can decrease sexual interest or, at times, cause impotence. Obviously, there are many occasions when patients with high blood pressure have to take these drugs, and the doctor's recommendations *must* be followed despite the side effects, but you should discuss these effects with him freely. Though we know less about the effects of drugs on female sexuality, we assume that drugs adversely affecting men affect women similarly.

Most people do not realize that alcohol, too, is a drug. Pharmacologically, it is a depressant and not a stimulant, though in small amounts it may relax sexual inhibition in a pleasant manner. In larger amounts, however, it usually interferes with sexual performance, reducing potency in males and orgasmic ability in females. At the very least, alcohol often produces drowsiness when a couple goes to bed for sex. The excessive use of alcohol is a frequent and too little recognized factor in sexual problems among the old. A very important aspect of this is failure to realize how much one is actually drinking. As an example, a man of sixty-four gives a history which strongly suggests the involvement of alcohol in his sexual problems:

I have been a heavy drinker all my life but I do not consider myself to be an alcoholic. I enjoy every bit of my life except my sexual relationship with my wife. I have the urge but not the erection, making it impossible for normal intercourse.

People should remember that the tolerance for alcohol decreases with age (one reason for this is changing kidney excretory power) so that smaller and smaller amounts may begin to produce negative effects. Older persons who choose to drink should limit themselves to a *maximum* of 1½ ounces of hard liquor, two 6-ounce glasses of wine, or three 8-ounce glasses of beer in any twenty-four-hour period. Remember, too, that alcohol is very dangerous in combination with narcotic and nonnarcotic drugs such as sleeping pills, sedatives, painkillers, antihistamines or tranquilizers, because it can pyramid their effects. Do not drink if you are taking drugs without discussing it with your doctor.

Tobacco is also a drug because of its nicotine content, although not usually categorized as one, and it may be a factor in impotence. Toxic changes in the blood from nicotine may affect the hormones.

Regular users of barbiturates as sedatives and hypnotics (sleeping pills) may become impotent.

Habitual users of opiates like morphine and heroin are often sexually impaired. Males who are addicted will usually be impotent.

Doctors should explain carefully to older patients the potential sexual side effects of drugs. In cases of serious illness, obviously, sexuality may have to be partially or even totally sacrificed for a period of time in order to obtain the beneficial effects of those drugs which are essential to treatment of the illness. But in many cases alternative drugs or other treatment can be given which have lesser or no effects on sexuality. For example, an antihypertensive drug that may adversely affect one person will not affect another. The possible sexual side effects of a drug should be balanced against the risks of the disease, and the patient's preference should be a factor in the decision. In our experience, numbers of men have become psychologically impotent because they misread the temporary effects of medications as signs of permanent sexual impairment. Other men attribute their impotence to aging rather than to drugs, and do not resume sexual activity even after the offending drugs have been removed. As one final point, we find that older people, both men and women, tend to need fewer tranquilizers and antidepressants as their sexual activity and sexual satisfaction increase.

4

Common Emotional Problems with Sex

Sexual problems you have in the later years may be caused by upsetting events in your life, such as the death of a loved one, retirement, marital conflicts, or simply too much stress and worry. Growing older itself can be frightening, especially if you don't know what to expect or how to handle it. Your early life experience and your society's attitudes have their impact as well.

A major emotional problem for the older man is the *fear* of sexual impotence. Some men have to deal with actual impotence, which is usually temporary. *Impotence occurs occasionally in nearly all men of all ages* for a variety of reasons — among

88

them fatigue, tension, illnesses and excessive drinking. In most cases potency returns by itself without specific treatment when the causative physical or emotional condition is reversed. In later life, however, certain men do begin to have chronic difficulty in obtaining and maintaining an erection. Some find that their capacity for sexual intercourse is greatly diminished and others cannot make love at all. We discussed the possible organic causes of impotence in Chapter 3. But the great majority of problems are psychologically caused. The male penis is a barometer of a man's feelings and quickly reflects his state of mind and his current life situation. The nerve connections that control the penis are extremely sensitive to emotions. Anxiety, fear and anger are the primary feelings that can cause a man to lose an erection rapidly or fail to achieve one in the first place. A disturbance in sexual functioning is often one of the first indications of unusual stress or emotional problems.

Men who do not know about the *normal* physiological changes in their sexual behavior that come with aging may believe falsely that they are becoming impotent. The expectation of high performance which is taught to males from childhood on through constant emphasis on competition and winning leads many men to overemphasize the physical-performance aspect of their sexuality. They may become more concerned about erections and ejaculations and less about expressing their feelings. This makes impotence or even its threat greatly upsetting. The *fear* of impotence can *cause* impotence. The harder a man tries to have an erection, the less likely he is to succeed. Impotence does not respond to will power and force. If it is truly transitory, it is much more likely to improve with relaxation and freedom from pressure.

Unresponsive sexual partners can threaten men and lead to impotence. A wife's disinterest or perfunctory acquiescence is very likely to affect her husband. Women may also become impatient or demanding, and make a transitory potency problem more severe. Some find impotence threatening to their own self-esteem and react with hostility or hurt. They see it as a sign of disinterest in them or a failure on their part to be sexually attractive.

Emotional and physical fatigue, boredom with routine love-making, overwork, and worries about family or finances can all affect potency. Impotence is often one of the first symptoms of depression. Disappointment, sadness and grief over personal losses can be a factor. So can resentfulness and irritation.

Sometimes impotence is a result of hidden fear of death or injury. Fred Patterson, a businessman and retired Army officer, had been a vigorous and sexually active man until he suffered a coronary attack four years ago. After the attack he was unable to have an erection. It took many sessions with a psychiatrist to help him recognize that his fear that sexual activity might bring on another coronary was the reason he did not allow himself to have an erection. His doctor agreed to a provisional program of exercise, including sex, which would not jeopardize his heart. As Patterson's anxiety lessened through psychotherapeutic counseling, and his sense of well-being increased following his physical fitness program, his sexual ability returned.

A sudden attack of impotence is likely to be the result of some unusual stress, and will usually abate when the stress is relieved. If impotence continues for any considerable period of time, information and reassurance from a doctor or professional counselor may be all that is needed. If the impotence still persists, however, comprehensive medical evaluation and more extended psychotherapy and/or sexual counseling may be required. The cooperation and support of one's partner are important in overcoming impotence. Even long-term impotence is not hopeless. Havelock Ellis, the well-known British psychologist and sexologist, overcame his lifelong impotence for the first time in old age. He did it without professional help, through a relationship with a sensitive, loving woman who was new to his life.

Women are somewhat less subject to fear of sexual dysfunctioning in later life than men, largely because they do not have to worry about erection. The normal physical changes that accompany aging interfere little with female sexual ability. Unlike most men, women can perform the sex act even when they are emotionally upset or uninterested. They may not enjoy love-making or have an orgasm in such situations, but they are physically capable of having intercourse. (They may, however, worry about orgasmic capacity, much as men are concerned about erection and ejaculatory capacity.) Indeed, in later life some women become more relaxed about sex and may even come to enjoy it more now that the menopause has freed them from fears of unwanted pregnancies. Their responsibilities diminish when their children leave home, and the "empty nest" is frequently a welcome event rather than a problem.

But women can have other problems. Many older men and women grew up believing that "nice" women were not interested in sex and indeed found it distasteful. They were traditionally admonished or conditioned to be passive, resigned and accepting; it was "loose" women who gave themselves to the pleasures of sex or sought it. A nineteenth-century marriage manual advised: "As a general rule, a modest woman seldom desires any sexual gratification for herself. She submits to her husband, but only to please him; and, but for the desire of maternity, would far rather be relieved from his attentions." Women may remember being taught that sex was simply a duty. Men were the pursuers, women reluctant and pursued. Such ingrained attitudes interfere with the development of close relationships in which partners share openly in the enjoyment of sex. If this has been your experience, frank talks with your partner can help clear up antiquated assumptions. It will often be easier than you think to talk freely about this, so give it a try.

The most profound emotional and sexual difficulties for older women revolve around the possibility of finding themselves alone — widowed, divorced, separated or single — as they grow older. Their lives are affected by one major fact: there are not enough men to go around. In the United States in 1970 there were more than eight million men aged sixty-five or over and more than eleven million women.* This disparity increases year by year as time passes, for two reasons. First, women outlive men by an average of seven years. (In 1970 life expectancy from birth was 74.9 years for females and 67.5 years for males.†) Second, women marry men an average of three years older than themselves.

Anticipating this loneliness, women find the first signs of gray hair and wrinkles in the late thirties and forties to be uneasy portents of things to come. Some of them become preoccupied with their physical appearance and fear the loss of youthful attractiveness. It is unfair to write off such apprehension as vanity or a "menopausal symptom." It would be easier for them to

---

*Of the eleven million women over sixty-five, over six million were widows and an additional 1.2 million were divorced or single. (About 7 percent of all older women had never married.)

†As one grows older these figures change, and life expectancy increases. *On the average,* a man of sixty-five can expect another thirteen years and a woman sixteen years.

adjust to the physical changes of growing older if the life spans of men and women were equal and if they were not stigmatized by the emphasis our culture places on youth.

But women do not have to collaborate with society's attitudes. The older woman should not give up her chance for a new relationship following widowhood or divorce. Older men can freely date and marry women of all ages, but social attitudes still tend to restrict women to socializing within their own age group. A woman who goes out with a younger man risks ridicule, but more women are beginning to take that risk. Remember also that, despite apparently discouraging statistics, up to the age of seventy-five there are still 100 men for every 130 women.

PROBLEMS BETWEEN SEXUAL PARTNERS

Sexual problems can reflect a troubled relationship between partners or can be its cause. Older couples often complain that they feel mismatched sexually because they have different needs and desires. But sexual partners seldom have exactly the same sexual desires, whatever their age. There are individual neurophysiological differences from birth. Inhibitions implanted during early sexual development will affect one person more than another. The amount of daily stimulation differs between partners; most commonly, the man who works is likely to be in contact with other women while the wife is more restricted at home. Whatever the reason for problems, the question is whether differences in needs are too great to reconcile or whether compromise and cooperation can work.

Sex can become a means to express anger, and even destructive feelings, between older people or toward oneself or the world at large, just as it can for younger people. Some relationships are kept alive through the use of sex to manipulate or intimidate. The passive partner in such a relationship has contributed to the problem by allowing the situation to continue, sometimes for years.

Couples may also withhold sex from each other in order to punish or control. Don't let yourself fall into this pattern. Talk problems out instead of going along with the old ruse, "Not tonight, dear, I have a headache." Sexual refusal is commonly thought of as a weapon used by controlling women, or by women too passive to fight openly. Less well known is the fact that the impotence of some men is their way of angrily rejecting women.

Retirement can cause serious problems. After all, twenty-four hours a day of togetherness is difficult for anyone of any age. Such unremitting intimacy places greater pressure on emotional relationships and brings problems into more acute focus. Even if you have enjoyed each other and looked forward to retirement, this constant proximity may dismay or disconcert or irritate you. It is essential that you work out a balance between shared time and time alone to give each of you elbow room.

Sexual boredom is very common among older married couples, who tend to fall into routine patterns in which they do the same old thing sexually time after time, year after year, with little imagination in technique or style and no zest for creating sexual excitement. The partners may no longer even care for each other. Sex with a new partner may bring improvement, but unless the sources of underlying boredom are dealt with, the improvement may prove only temporary once the novelty has worn off.

Time itself is a factor, especially in a relationship that has lasted thirty or forty or fifty years, not only because of sexual boredom but because long-standing problems sometimes worsen as the result of chronic irritation from years of unresolved conflict. (Interestingly, marriages which were unstable and unsatisfactory earlier in life sometimes improve in the later years as the children grow up and leave, and the stresses of parenthood and career pass.) Partners frequently change in personality and interests over time. These changes may move them in noncomplementary directions, producing two people who no longer love or even like each other or whose interests now diverge widely. Sometimes only one partner changes, while the other, uninterested in change, becomes resentful about what is happening. All these tensions erode a marital relationship.

Illness may incapacitate one sexual partner but not the other. Frequently the man develops serious illnesses first, leaving the woman without a sexual partner. Healthy women — especially those who are significantly younger than their husbands — may spend years in a marital relationship without sex. Other feelings also complicate the sexual picture. If one partner becomes ill, the other ordinarily reacts with concern and a desire to help, but if the illness becomes chronic, the well partner may be surprised to find himself or herself angry at the sick one. This may reflect threat of the possible loss of the other; it can also represent overwork and exhaustion; or it can indicate resentment over missing out on things or being tied down to a nursing role. In order not to feel guilty about these understandable resentments, face them frankly and secure some outside help from your relatives, neighbors, friends, or professional homemakers to reduce the burden.

We sometimes see older marriage in which the man has always assumed a predominately fatherly, protective role toward his more dependent wife. He may call her "my baby" or "little girl" even in later life. If he becomes ill and requires her care, serious problems, including sexual difficulties, can arise. The wife, who has always been babied, can become petulant, dissatisfied or simply unable or unwilling to play a giving and responsive role. A variant of this is the hypochondriacal man — the worrywart — married to an independent and caretaking wife who becomes ill. When she cannot mother her husband, the equilibrium in which they had functioned for so long is upset.

Disfigurements caused by illnesses, as well as physical changes associated with age, can affect the marital relationship. One or both partners may be repelled or embarrassed by varicose veins, hearing problems or Parkinsonism. Wrinkled or loose skin, gray hair, "liver spots" and other visible accompaniments of disease and aging are intolerable to some people's concept of sexuality.

And some older people make themselves unnecessarily unattractive. Sloppy hygiene, old wrappers and nightclothes, hair curlers, failure to shave daily, and similar habits are signals to a partner that one no longer cares about his or her sensibilities.

What should you do if you and your partner are having sexual and marital problems? First talk to each other about the problems — often. It is important to determine the basis of the problem and then to cooperate with each other in attempting to resolve it. Be prepared for the fact that each of you may refuse to admit your own contribution to the situation and may project the blame onto the other. It is difficult to be open and objective about emotional issues. But it is absolutely imperative to realize that what you should be looking for is a solution rather than a culprit. If you find you need help, go together to your clergyman, physician or a professional psychotherapist or counselor. If your partner won't go, go alone. Late-life separation and divorce is the very last resort. It is an extremely painful and jolting experience, and all efforts should be made to salvage and improve even the most difficult relationships.

Younger persons should know that many of the sexual problems found in old age begin in the middle years, when they are preoccupied with raising a family, earning a living and perhaps caring for older family members. The responsibility for both ends of the life cycle often rests on them. Under these pressures there is too little time left to pay much attention to marital and sexual relationships, so these tend to be neglected. Busyness can mask the lack of communication, and this failure can prove serious when the couple is older and begins to spend more time together.

WIDOWHOOD AND GRIEF

The losses and grieving that are inevitable in the emotional lives of all older people need to be worked through and accepted, in order that the survivor be freed psychologically to resume a full life or shape a new and different one. Losing someone you have loved — spouse, partner, friend, child — usually means shock and then a long, slow journey through grief. Acute grief, with intense mental anguish and remorse, ordinarily lasts a month or two and then begins to lessen. In most cases grief works itself out in six to eighteen months unless it is complicated by further loss, stress or other factors. *Widow shock,* an exaggerated state which can follow the sudden and unexpected death of a partner or occur when the surviving partner is ill prepared to handle living alone, leaves the survivor unable to accept death and take up life again. To recover, he or she needs to be encouraged to grieve and should be given assistance in building an active life once more. The open expression of feelings, including crying, is important for both men and women in resolving grief. Sharing one's sadness, anger, resentment, fear and self-pity with someone helps.

Such *grief work* also involves talking about your sexual feelings. People need to separate out their own identities from the previous commingling of identities that occurs in close and long-term relationships. The feeling that "part of me died with him (or her)" can then be replaced with the feeling that "I am a person in myself and I am still alive."

Anticipatory grief, during which a person undergoes an extended grief reaction prior to the expected death of the loved one — as happens in the course of a terminal illness — can soften the shock of death. Such grieving may result in a closer relationship with the ill spouse, but there are also instances when the grieving person may close himself or herself off as though the spouse were already dead. When this occurs, outside help may be needed to re-establish the relationship with the dying person.

Sometimes the death of a spouse causes the survivor to stop the action. In *enshrinement* the survivor keeps things just as they were when the loved one was alive and spends his or her energy revering the memory of the dead person, surrounded by photographs and rooms kept intact. The survivor thinks that to live fully is a betrayal of love or loyalty for the dead. This survival guilt and fear of infidelity lead to emotional stagnation and stand in the way of achieving new relationships. The usual cure for enshrinement is to take an active role in getting life moving again. This is an act of will and determination. It can happen only if the individual decides to make it happen. It will also help to remove from sight the personal possessions of the deceased.

If grief and anger over a death continue unchanged over a period of years, something is interfering with the natural healing process of time. Quite often it is unresolved negative feelings toward the dead person, as in an unhappy marriage, or a stubborn refusal to accept fate (an adult temper tantrum) and to take positive steps toward creating a new life. In these cases, professional help may be necessary.

TRAPS TO LOOK OUT FOR

Even when their physical and mental health is excellent, men and women in their fifties, sixties and seventies sometimes exhibit an old-man or old-woman act as though they were tottering invalids on their last legs. Having a rigid, stereotyped desexualized image of what an older person *should* be, they play the role with stubborn determination. The "old-person act" allows them to avoid responsibility toward themselves and others and to evoke sympathy. It is a symptom of demoralization and giving up.

Certain older persons decide that sexual ability is gone and arbitrarily declare themselves sexually incapacitated. Angry or obstinate refusal to discuss the issue with the partner or to consider possible remedies is typical in these instances. Behind this stance is an effort to avoid anxiety about sex or a sexual relationship.

Some older people decide they are ugly and undesirable and begin to hate the way they look. They make frantic attempts to appear young but may become depressed over the hopelessness of altering their appearance significantly. Another variation of self-hatred is found in those people who look into the mirror and insist that what they see "is not the real me." They may decide that their only true self is interior and refuse to accept or identify with their physical characteristics. Although it may take some time to accomplish this, it is essential to accept as part of one's self the realities of change.

Sometimes the angry response of older people to their own sexual and social deprivation is hostility toward those who are younger. Everyone has heard bitter threats such as "You'll see what it's like when *you're* old" or "Wait until you reach *my* age — you won't be so smart." There may also be self-righteous criticism of the sexuality of their own contemporaries as well as of the young.

Many older men and women make a self-fulfilling prophecy of sexual failure. Overwhelmed and demoralized by the unattractive picture drawn by society of late life, they literally give up without trying, or guarantee their own failure when they do try. To anticipate failure is to cause it to happen. If you think yourself unattractive, you tend to become so. If you believe you are sexually ineligible, you are likely to hide yourself away from opportunities that might lead to social and sexual encounters.

SEXUAL GUILT AND SHAME

Sexual guilt and shame are factors in many people's reaction to sex. These feelings derive from childhood and family experiences, and from the sexual searchings of childhood, which are so often confusing and disturbing. People past sixty, often brought up in a period of Victorian-like prudery, are likely to have been treated to more than their share of misinformation, made to feel guilty about any sexual stirrings they sensed, and given few chances to get satisfying answers to their questions — if they dared ask them. The culture insisted that childhood was innocent of sexuality, and any normal expression of it, verbal or physical — looking, feeling, talking, touching — was often punished.

Masturbation was strictly forbidden. The Victorians invented a grotesque array of mechanical devices to make certain that children, particularly boys, would not be able to stimulate themselves. Children were warned that masturbation could cause feeble-mindedness or madness; it could "use up the life juices," weaken the body and shorten the life span, and make one nervous, distracted and highstrung. Dark circles under the eyes were alleged indications of secret masturbation, and a grisly folklore sprang up in which hands withered and fell off if they were used in sexual stimulation.

An important misassumption that many older men still have from their youth is that "too much" sexual activity reduces potency and lowers semen "reserves." The belief that semen must be conserved is sheer nonsense because it is constantly produced — yet in 1937 a sex hygiene manual from the U.S. Public Health Service was still warning youths not to "waste vital fluids" and the 1945 edition of the *Boy Scout Manual* repeated these words.

Because for older men and women the greater part of their procreative years occurred before birth control techniques were as sophisticated, reliable and freely available as they are today, spontaneous sexual enjoyment was often hampered by the fear of pregnancy. Chronic and justified fears of venereal disease, for which effective drugs had not yet been devised, also laid psychological inhibitions on sexuality. So did many traditional religious teachings.

The habit-forming effects of such long-term constraints tend to linger, and it is often hard for older people to give themselves freely and impulsively to sexual expression. It is not easy to overcome ingrained guilt and shame even when you in your better judgment know that sexuality need no longer be considered evil or dangerous. Thinking through your own childhood and early adult experiences may help you understand your present feelings better. Remember once again that sexual problems, whether caused by personal or by social factors, are rarely insurmountable.

5

Do Yourself a Favor

Sex, one of the great free and renewable pleasures of life, does not take kindly to sloth and apathy. To get the most out of sex you will do yourself a favor if you are in shape for it. Two powerful aphrodisiacs that have been certified effective are a vigorous and well-cared-for body and a lively personality. Much can be done to preserve the functioning of both. We shall be talking here specifically about your body.

FITNESS FOR OLDER PEOPLE

The enjoyment of sex is enhanced by a fairly healthy, fairly pain-free body. Apart from visits to the doctor for a specific complaint, older men and women ideally should have a physical examination every year. Women should also have a gynecological examination every six months, particularly to check for breast and vaginal cancer. Any problems in sexual functioning should be brought to the doctor's attention at the time of these examinations, if not at a special appointment in between. The purpose of all this is to detect and treat physical problems in their early stages and to provide the medical basis for a program of preventive health care, including exercise, nutrition and rest.

Exercise. An exercise program can improve physical appearance and increase longevity. It is crucial for a healthy heart, arteries and respiratory system and has a relaxing effect on the nervous system. Studies indicate that bones will stay bigger and stronger during aging if one exercises regularly. In addition, exercise can improve one's sex life. The only bad news is that it requires discipline and a certain amount of work. Exercise should be planned on a routine and daily basis. If you decide to undertake it, you simply make time for it. According to a study by the President's Council on Physical Fitness and Sports, 45 percent of all Americans do not exercise at all, and older people exercise less than younger people. This is unfortunate since the older you are, the more help your body needs from you.

Physical fitness is a quality of life, a condition of looking and feeling well and having the necessary physical reserves to enjoy a range of interests, among which is sex. It has two components. Basic health or *organic fitness* means a well-nourished body as free as possible from disease or infirmity. If there are physical limitations, they will have been compensated for to the greatest degree possible. The second component, called *dynamic fitness,* means that a person is not simply free from disease but fully fit to move vigorously and energetically. This involves efficiency of heart and lungs, muscular strength and endurance, balance, flexibility, coordination and agility.

Two distinct kinds of exercise are necessary: one to keep the body limber and supple and strengthen the muscles, the other to increase endurance and enlarge the heart capacity. Any number of excellent books give guidance on exercise. Especially relevant to older people is a booklet called *The Fitness Challenge in the Later Years,* prepared jointly by the Administration on Aging and the President's Council on Physical Fitness and Sports.* This describes a reasonable level of exercise, starting at first very slowly and moving up at your own speed. There are pre-exercise tests, warm-up exercises and ''interval training'' instructions, where you gradually tax your body, little by little, until you reach a certain level of performance. It is

*DHEW Publication No. (OHD/AOA) 73 - 20802, May, 1968 (reprinted November, 1973). Available for 70 cents from U.S. Department of Health, Education and Welfare, Office of Human Development, Administration on Aging, Washington, D.C. 20201.

recommended that you discuss your exercise program with your own doctor and ask him or her to advise you. There are wide variations in physical performances and capacities. Your own individual physical condition should determine your appropriate exercises, and their level and pace. If you become temporarily ill or inactive, you will usually need to return to an earlier level of activity and slowly work your way back. In all cases avoid strenuous bursts of sudden activity when you are out of shape.

Brisk walking is a good all-around exercise for older people, accompanied by a regimen of calisthenics. The squeezing action of the leg muscles on the veins during walking helps promote the return of blood on its way back to the heart. Start out by walking rapidly until you begin to feel tired. Rest and walk back to your starting point. Keep doing this, for longer distances, until you reach a reasonable goal (which may take a year or so if you have previously been idle), such as a walk of two to three miles a day in forty-five minutes. Jogging, swimming and other more vigorous activities can be preceded by a treadmill stress test (available in many hospitals), especially if you have been inactive or there has ever been indication of possible heart disease. As a supplement to a regular program of exercise, older persons should take advantage of any opportunity for physical movement — walking upstairs, doing chores, mowing the lawn, gardening, dancing: in short, bending, stretching and moving as much as possible.

Dr. Theodore G. Klumpp, consultant to the President's Council on Physical Fitness and Sports, remarks on the fact that many people won't exercise for fear that it will provoke a heart attack. But "exercise opposes the effect of stroke or heart attack," he notes. "Blood clots form when the blood is sluggish rather than when it is vigorous." Even those persons who have already had heart attacks are usually placed on an exercise program by their physicians shortly after initial recovery in order to reduce the possibility of another attack.

Exercising Your Trouble Spots. There

are specific exercises which can greatly improve the appearance of the older person if undertaken on a regular basis:

For a *double chin* or *sagging neck,* sit or stand as tall as possible, top of head reaching toward ceiling, then slowly roll head in a circle, trying to touch right shoulder, back, left shoulder and chest as your head rotates. Do this daily, first in a clockwise direction, then counterclockwise, ten times. Use a slow, smooth motion. Keep your eyes open to avoid getting dizzy and losing your balance.

A *potbelly* can be controlled by lying flat on your back on the floor, legs straight, arms at sides, and curling your head and shoulders as far off the floor as you can, holding this position for five counts. Do this ten or fifteen times a day. You will feel your stomach muscles tighten as you lift off the floor. As you get stronger you can try lifting your legs off the floor rather than your head, as long as you do not arch your back. Keep your knees straight, hold your feet at an angle, lift and then slowly lower your legs. Repeat several times.

Improving *back muscles* will also help

your stomach muscles as well as preventing or alleviating back pain. As much as 80 percent of backaches are due to muscle fatigue rather than slipped discs or arthritis. Lie on your back, squeeze your buttocks together and tighten stomach muscles while flattening your back against the floor. Hold for a count of five, then relax and repeat ten times.

Flabby thighs can be conditioned by lying down on your left side on the floor, with your left arm stretched out and your right hand on the floor in front of your chest. Slowly swing your right leg directly up as high as possible, then lower to the starting position. Repeat until you feel mild fatigue in your thigh muscles. Then roll to the right side and repeat with your left leg.

To firm up your *upper arm,* stand facing the wall a little more than arm's length away. Then lean forward, putting hands against the wall shoulder high, keeping arms straight and supporting your body weight. Bend elbows until your forehead touches the wall. Then straighten arms and push your body back to starting position. Continue back and forth ten times.

Women with *sagging breasts* can improve chest muscles through swimming or exercises such as swinging the arms in large circles. Firm chest muscles will prevent round-shoulderedness and a hollow-chested appearance. Because there are no muscles holding up the breasts themselves, exercise will not help them, but a good bra will give support, and standing up straight can improve appearance.

There is also no exercise to improve the *sagging testicles* found in older men as the skin becomes less firm. Athletic supporters offer sufficient protection for vigorous activity.

In later years many women develop *weakened pelvic muscles,* which makes them feel the vagina is losing its ability to grip a penis. The Kegel exercises for women consist of twenty to thirty contractions of the muscles of the pelvic floor, as though one were holding oneself back from urinating and defecating at the same time. If the woman inserts one or two fingers into her vagina while doing the exercises, she can feel it tightening. These exercises should be performed several times daily and can be done while in a sitting or standing position and while you are doing other work. Contractions are held for only a few seconds, and the process must be repeated daily for at least one hundred contractions for the Kegel exercises to be truly effective.

When there is improved muscle tone as a result of using Kegel's exercises, the vaginal walls exert greater pressure on the penis. This is of particular value in those older couples where the man's penis has become somewhat smaller and the woman's vagina larger. Some women are able to use the Kegel movement in a rhythmic fashion during sexual intercourse, increasing the satisfaction to both partners. The exercises also help to support the pelvic structure — the uterus, bladder and rectum.

Nutrition. If you are over sixty, beware of poor nutrition and even malnutrition. You may protest, "But that's absurd! I've always eaten a normal diet." But poor nutrition sneaks up on you in later life. Medical and lay people alike share the illusion that the United States is the world's best-fed nation. This is not true, and it is especially not true for older persons. There are many reasons for this, the most obvious being the rising cost of good-quality food and the lowered incomes of many people as they grow older. But there are other, less obvious reasons. Social isolation and depression can cause people to lose their appetites and stop taking an interest in cooking; physical limitations may make shopping and preparing food difficult; loss of teeth or poor teeth interfere with eating solid foods; illnesses, alcoholism and chronic diseases of many kinds can affect food consumption; and finally poor eating habits may develop (snacking, the tea-and-toast syndrome, junk and convenience foods like TV dinners). Persons who live alone are especially prone to neglect proper diets — "It's too much bother to fix a meal for just one person."

What are the dangers of poor nutrition? You become more vulnerable to disease. You fatigue more easily and lose a sense of well-being. You are more likely to have emotional problems, among them depression, apathy, anxiety. Age-related processes can be accelerated, and sexual interest and performance are often lowered. Thus you have a great many reasons to eat well aside from the well-known pleasures of food itself.

A healthy diet includes three kinds of foods — proteins (meat, dairy products, eggs, fish, poultry, beans, nuts and some grains), carbohydrates (cereals, breads, pastries, vegetables, fruits), and fats (meat, dairy products, oils, nuts and grains). Carbohydrates are the cheapest foods, and both sweettooths, who love sugar, and people on low budgets, who find starchy foods filling, may overload their diets with them. Starches, sugar and other sweeteners fill the stomach, raise the blood sugar, lower the appetite and lead to a false sense of well-being. Do not be deceived. You must have some of the relatively more expensive proteins every day for vitality and body-tissue repair. If cost is a problem, learn more about preparing foods "from scratch," using lower-cost proteins (dried skim milk, dried beans, cheaper cuts of meat, etc.). The home economics departments of high schools or colleges near you can offer advice, as will the U.S. Department of Agriculture, Washington, D.C. In general, cut down on desserts, pastries, fat meats, gravies, beer, sweet wines, hard liquors and soft drinks. Natural sources of sugar, like frozen orange juice, are better for you and cheaper than many other products made from refined white sugar. Use those vegetable oils and margarines low in saturated fats and less butter, lard, cream and margarines high in saturated fats.*

If you happen to be overweight and need to diet, a useful book to buy or borrow is Consumers Guide's *Rating the Diets* by

---

*The following food booklets are all available from the Superintendent of Documents, Government Printing Office, Washington, D.C. 20402:

Your Money's Worth in Foods (50¢)
Calories and Weight ($1.00)
Fats in Food and Diet (30¢)
Cooking for Two ($1.25)
Food Guide for Older Folks (40¢)
Nutrition: Food at Work for You (40¢)

Single copies of a booklet entitled *Food Is More Than Just Something to Eat* are available from Nutrition, Pueblo, Colorado 81009.

Theodore Berland and the editors of Consumers Guide, 3323 West Main Street, Skokie, Illinois 60076 ($2.50), which gives you the pros and cons of all the popular diets as well as valuable information on food and health. Avoid crash and fad diets since they can harm your health and your appearance. Pick a diet you can live comfortably with in good health while still losing weight. Diet clubs such as TOPS, Weight Watchers, Overeaters Anonymous or self-organized weight clubs can make it easier for people with persistent weight problems to lose weight.

Diets aimed at prevention of disease are important far before age sixty. We know a good deal, for example, about diet and the prevention of heart disease. The granddaddy of heart-disease-prevention diets is the Prudent Man's Diet, devised by Dr. Norman Jolliffe in 1957, which is still being revised and updated regularly. This is a balanced, low-calorie diet which lowers the amount of saturated fats and cholesterol you eat.* It calls for a total of 2,400 calories a day (compared to the American average of 3,200), with no more than 35 percent fat in the diet, increased protein and a reduction of carbohydrates and salt. In addition to the books mentioned below, a free booklet of low-fat recipes and cooking advice can be obtained from local heart associations, or from the American Heart Association (44 East 23rd Street, New York, N.Y. 10010).

Other tips for older people:

• Go easy on salt since you are more susceptible to high blood pressure.

• Get bulk in your diet that is important for digestion by eating vegetables like raw celery, carrots, and whole-grain bread and cereals. This is true for all older people but especially for those who are dieting to lose weight. Bran cereal is good. If you want lots of bulk at low cost, buy coarse bran

---

*Two current examples of cookbooks based on these principles are *The American Heart Association Cookbook,* New York: David McKay, 1973, and Lawrence Lamb's *What You Need to Know About Food and Cooking for Health,* New York: Viking, 1973. Another excellent cookbook is *The Jack Sprat Cookbook; or Good Eating on a Low-Cholesterol Diet,* by Polly Zane, New York: Harper & Row, 1973.

(local health-food stores usually carry it) for a few cents a pound. If you don't live near a health-food store, get a mail-order health-food catalogue. Coarse bran tastes like a cross between babies' pablum and sawdust, but if you take several teaspoonfuls in between swallows of fruit juice at each meal or a larger amount on your breakfast cereal daily, you will be taking an important step in promoting good bowel action and preventing diverticulosis, certain kinds of constipation and other bowel problems. Bran is far better for you than laxatives. Doctors used to prescribe low-residue (limited-bulk) diets for older people with bowel problems, but just the opposite is now generally true.

• Try to avoid getting into the habit of taking laxatives, which can in fact induce habitual constipation. As we have noted, a good diet with plenty of bulk and plenty of exercise are the best ways to prevent constipation in later life. If you do need an occasional laxative, many doctors feel that milk of magnesia is preferable to mineral oil, which tends to reduce the absorption of fat-soluble vitamins.

- "Indigestion" from eating fried foods may mean gallstones; consult your doctor. Some liver specialists believe that a low-fat diet can help prevent formation of gallstones.
- Gout, arthritis, diabetes and a number of other diseases which can directly affect your sex life as well as your general health may require a special diet prescribed by your doctor.
- Some overweight people, more often women than men, have a bumpy kind of fat known as cellulite on their thighs and hips that resembles the texture of the skin of an orange. It can hang from upper arms or droop around the stomach. Often dieting alone will not remove it. The best known technique thus far for getting rid of this bothersome fat is exercise and, especially, direct, vigorous massage of the affected area on a regular basis. You can do this yourself or ask your partner to do it.
- If you tend to neglect your nutrition or are under stress, take a standard vitamin and mineral supplement to supply the minimum daily requirement.
- Anemia may occur when your diet is

inadequate in iron and protein. Foods containing iron are lean meats, dark green leafy vegetables, whole grain and enriched breads and cereals. The dietary approach is more economical and just as effective as the highly advertised vitamin and mineral preparations. (Remember that anemia should be evaluated by your doctor.)

• Osteoporosis is the gradual softening of the bones, which can lead to deformities and easy bone breakage. Prevention of this disease should begin in middle age by eating adequate but not excessive protein, getting sufficient calcium from milk and milk products like cheese and yoghurt, and by regular physical exercise. If you suspect you have osteoporosis, check with your doctor, who may prescribe a specific regimen.

• Large doses of Vitamin E have been recommended for a variety of disorders, including sterility and vascular diseases and for retarding the aging process, curing impotence and healing wounds and burns. There is as yet no convincing scientific evidence for these claims. The recommended daily allowance for women is 20 IU to 25 IU and for men, 30 IU.

However, there have been no reports of toxic effects even when very large daily doses are taken for months. Therefore, it appears that you can take a lot of Vitamin E without hurting yourself but with no assurance that large doses will help any common physical disorder.

• In general, be prudent about taking over-the-counter medications widely advertised on television and radio; they are sometimes valueless, often costly, and on occasion — especially if you take them in large quantities or combine them — hazardous. An office visit to your doctor may prove less expensive, as well as better for your health, than self-diagnosis and self-administered remedies for a physical complaint.

It is a common belief that people need fewer calories as they grow older. One source claims that your body will require 10 percent fewer calories between ages thirty-five and fifty-five than when you were under thirty-five, 16 percent fewer between ages fifty-five and seventy-five, and one percent fewer calories per year for every year over seventy-five. We are not totally convinced. We suspect that this theory is based on the fact that many older people become less active and fail to work or exercise their bodies, and that caloric needs are a function of activity and not of age. Some inactivity is of course related to physical ailments, but much more is simply lack of motivation and inertia. The older you get, the more temptation you will feel to take it easy. Remember the maxim, "Most people don't wear out, they rust out." Lack of movement leads to poor appetite, which in turn leads to fatigue and a vicious cycle.

You will find that you feel and sleep better if you make your evening meal relatively light. (Breakfast is a good time to eat heartily.) Cutting down on food and alcohol intake before bed is also conducive to better sex. If you have had a heavy evening meal, it is best to postpone sex for a few hours to avoid unnecessary strain on the heart and other organs.

Rest. A rested body enhances sexual desire and improves sexual performance as well as contributing to general health and well-being. Contrary to general opinion, as you grow older you will need as much or more sleep than when you were younger. You may, however, notice changes in your sleep patterns. Studies show that older people seem to experience less "deep" or "delta" sleep (the period of dreamless oblivion) and become "lighter" sleepers, with more frequent awakenings. In addition, depression, anxiety, grief, loneliness and lack of exercise can affect sleep patterns and depth of sleep. Early-morning awakening is more common among the inactive, the depressed, those who go to bed early and those who take frequent cat naps during the day.

Get seven to ten hours' sleep per night according to your needs. This varies from person to person. More sleep is needed if you have physical health problems. Take one or more naps or rest breaks during the day and stretch out in bed.

If insomnia strikes, don't panic. To prepare for sleep, avoid strong coffee before bedtime since caffeine can keep you awake. Decaffeinated coffee is preferrable. The establishment of simple rituals can get you psychologically ready for sleep: warm baths, a well-made, firm and comfortable bed and pillows, back massage by a partner, reading a book, watching TV or listening to music. Often warm milk, one glass of wine, a soothing talk with your partner or a phone call to an understanding friend can comfort you and relax your tensions.

Bedtime is a time when your defenses against anxiety, anger and other emotions are down. If these create persistent troubled sleep or insomnia, psychotherapy or some form of counseling may help. Avoid nonprescription sleep remedies since they are expensive and largely useless. Eventually your body will become tired enough to sleep by itself. We don't recommend sleeping pills (hypnotics) unless you are in pain or great physical or emotional discomfort, because they can be habit-forming and may cause adverse side effects, including, paradoxically, the perpetuation of insomnia. The use of hypnotics should be evaluated by a physician on an ongoing basis. Prescriptions should not be automatically renewed time after time. Active, pleasurable sexual activity, including masturbation, can be an excellent sleep inducer. This effect is strongest when there is orgasm, but even without it such activity is usually mildly relaxing.

Hearing Problems. One out of every four older persons has a hearing impairment. For a number of reasons — among them embarrassment, false pride, a psychological determination to deny the fact — a surprising number of people refuse to use hearing aids even when they will help. Not all hearing impairments can be improved by wearing a hearing aid, but only an audiologist (a specialist trained in a program accredited by the American Speech and Hearing Association) or an otologist or otolaryngologist (doctors specifically trained to treat ear disorders) can determine this; and if you suspect you have some hearing loss, you should consult with one of these specialists. Remember, too, that hearing impairments tend to develop gradually, so you may be unaware this is happening to you. If you find yourself frequently missing parts of ordinary conversation around you or have trouble making out the dialogue when you go to the movies, it is a good idea to have your hearing checked.

Impaired hearing isolates one from society far more than most people realize. Present-day hearing aids are much less conspicuous, disfiguring and cumbersome than they used to be and observers are likely to be very matter-of-fact about them. If yours is the type of loss that can be compensated by the use of a hearing aid, do not let personal inhibitions stop you from using one. You will realize how much you have been missing only after your hearing improves.

It will take time for you to accustom yourself to a hearing aid, so be prepared for an adjustment period and stick with it despite discomfort at the start. You will probably find it helpful to watch how other people use their aids while you are learning to use yours. Thereafter, always use your aid whenever you are with another person.

You should be very careful to deal only with a responsible supplier. This is a field full of high-pressure door-to-door salesmen offering "low" prices, "easy" installment payments and defective or shoddy equipment. It is important that you be properly tested and fitted with an aid of good quality, appropriate to your needs.

People who have the kind of hearing loss that cannot be helped by a hearing aid must be frank with friends and intimates. It is unlikely that they will find this information embarrassing; the awkwardness is more likely to be on your side. Sit close to your companion so you can hear what is being said and speak up when you do not. It is only when one attempts to conceal a hearing impairment that problems are likely to arise.

THE AESTHETICS OF PERSONAL APPEARANCE

Older people notice how other older people look. So do younger people. Physical appearance is as important after sixty as at any other time. A wholesome vanity — pride in how you look to others — is a sign of healthy self-esteem, not of egotism. Unfortunately some older people who are otherwise in good health gradually become careless about the way they look without fully realizing it. A pleasing appearance does not require expensive clothes, but it does mean attention to the things that most other people notice: cleanliness, a reasonably trim figure, well-cared-for clothing, attention to hair, skin and nails, and the wise use of cosmetics. The most common complaints about appearance that we hear concern general sloppiness and even slovenliness. Women are bothered by older men's tendency to ignore their clothing, while a typical male complaint is that many older women neglect their hair, letting it become messy, or wear styles that are fussy, inappropriate or out-of-date. We want to offer a few brief tips on personal care that are particularly relevant to older people:

Skin Care for Men and Women.
Ideally, prevention of skin problems should begin in the early years for both men and women, but good skin care can help at any time in life. Skin can be damaged by too much sun or wind, and by malnutrition, excess alcohol, disease, depression, drugs and anxiety. Overexposure to the sun causes more premature aging, particularly

in Caucasians, than any other factor. Sunbathing and working or playing out of doors unprotected for long periods of time are the major culprits. They can result in permanent skin damage affecting both the outer and inner layers of skin, causing loss of water and elasticity, deep wrinkles and grooves. Prolonged exposure to very cold weather, overheated rooms with minimal humidity, and air conditioning in warm climates can deplete the moisture in the skin, making it look lined. Electric blankets left on all night can dry the body skin. Various kinds of air pollution can be damaging. Poor nutrition, whether vitamin deficiencies or unbalanced diets, can cause dry, scaly and inelastic skin. Sagging skin sometimes follows too rapid weight loss. Anxiety, depression and tension speed up the appearance of aging. Cigarette smoking can cause wrinkles to appear sooner than they normally would since nicotine narrows the small capillaries and cuts down the supply of blood bringing nourishment and oxygen to the skin.

Even with the best of preventive care, the human face begins to acquire noticeable lines and wrinkles around the age of forty. There is a gradual permanent loss of elasticity in both the skin and the underlying tissue. Wrinkles per se should not become an obsessive concern; "looking your age" does not mean looking unattractive. The facial changes of aging are aspects of individuality. But obviously all of us — even those not enmeshed in the cult of "youth" — want to look our best. Don't waste your money on "wrinkle removers" and other gimmicks "guaranteed" to make you look younger. Anything that keeps the skin moist will help to slow down the appearance of aging. We will describe a simple regimen which can be followed by those women and men who want to take care of their skin.

Thorough cleansing of the face and neck is important as the first step. Many older people can tolerate a mild soap like Ivory if it is used quickly and rinsed off completely. Neutrogena, which is much more expensive, can also be tried. Others may need to use a rinsable or washable cleanser which combines cream and a small amount of soap in lotion form. Facial Bath by Max

Factor is an example. (Creams and oils used alone are difficult to remove and the skin is never completely cleansed.) After cleansing and a thorough rinsing with warm water, the face should be patted dry and immediately protected by a light moisturizer by day or a heavier oily cream for night while the skin still holds moisture absorbed from the rinse. Most inexpensive dime-store creams work as well as expensive ones.* About once a week women should rub something rough on the face such as cleansing grains or inexpensive corn meal on a wet washcloth. This helps remove the outer layer of dry flaky cells. (Men need not do this since shaving accomplishes the same purpose.) The body itself can also be protected against drying by using a body lotion immediately after a bath or shower, when the skin has absorbed moisture.

Electric facial saunas dry the skin. The face should really not be massaged, but

*Cosmetics can be purchased at a reduced price through the pharmacy service provided for members of the American Association of Retired Persons. For information write NRTA-AARP Pharmacy, 1224 Twenty-fourth Street, N.W., Washington, D.C. 20037.

if you must do it, never stretch or pull the skin in any downward direction. Various chemical processes and dermabrasion (removal of the tissues of the outer skin layer with a rotating wire brush) can be dangerous unless done by skilled operators. They are also expensive. Plastic surgery (face lifts) for both men and women can correct severe skin sagging; but they, too, are expensive and good results last only three to five years. The best skin care is sensible cleansing, good diet, rest and lack of tension, and avoidance of too much sun, wind, alcohol or cigarettes.

Cleanliness. A surprising number of people become extremely careless about personal hygiene as they grow older. There are many possible reasons for this; it may be a sign of demoralization, of giving up, or an expression of anger at the rest of the world, or simple laziness and sloppiness. Not all cultures value cleanliness as ours does, and not all of *us* like cleanliness; we know one woman who said in a fury, "I'm not about to dress neatly and smell sweetly! At my age I've earned the right to be smelly if I choose." But if you are interested in a social life, you may as well face the fact that a daily bath or shower (during periods of illness a sponge bath can be substituted), a shave for men, regular tooth brushing (and well-fitting dentures) and cleanliness of hair, face, clothing and nails will improve your chances socially.

Hair Care. Many older people prefer to color gray or white hair, and this should be done carefully and subtly, paying attention to instructions, because the strong chemicals involved can damage hair otherwise. Actually, gray and white hair is very handsome, and it seems a pity that current fashion tends to reject it.

A number of people experience permanent thinning of their hair as they grow older. With women this may occur after menopause. Many men have a hereditary predilection toward baldness, but women seldom lose their hair to this extent except through illness. *Temporary* hair loss typically follows illness, poor diet or stress of any sort.

Healthy hair requires many of the same

elements as healthy skin — good nutrition, rest, absence of illness, protection from the elements. Simple cleansing with a mild shampoo such as Johnson's Baby Shampoo, thorough rinsing, and a pleasing hair style are all that is required for a head of hair that is already healthy. Dandruff can usually be controlled through various shampoos. You may need to shift brands occasionally to maintain effectiveness. Head and Shoulders, Selsun Blue, and Ionil T are three of the shampoos that work well. Severe scalp problems should be attended to by a professional dermatologist.

Many older people buy wigs and hairpieces. These are fine if they are natural-looking to begin with and are kept in good condition. But nothing looks worse than an older woman in a frizzy or bedraggled wig, or a man with an "obvious" hairpiece. If you cannot afford to buy and maintain a quality wig or hairpiece that cannot be detected from the real thing, stick to your own hair.

Cosmetics for Women. We have one piece of advice on cosmetics — go easy.

Cosmetics that were becoming when you were young are likely to be too harsh for your face later on, particularly heavy eye makeup and bright lipstick. Switch to gentler colors, which are much more flattering to older skin. Ask the honest advice of your family and friends, since you may be unable to notice that your makeup needs renovating. A moisturizer, a little accent or shading on the cheeks, some translucent powder, a subtle lipstick and perhaps a little enhancing eye makeup provide everything the older woman needs to look attractive.

Clothing. Older men and women tend to get into ruts with the clothing they wear. After years of marriage or single life they often forget the genuine aesthetic pleasure well-fitting and well-chosen clothing gives to others — and to oneself. Indeed, there are some older people who manifest an almost defiant, angry quality in their deliberate choice of inappropriate clothing. If you are on a tight budget and depend mostly on Social Security incomes and pensions, there is usually little room for the purchase of clothing. But when possible, it is morale building to acquire some new clothing on a regular basis. In some communities, thrift shops are a very good source of clothing; this will depend on where you live. If you cannot afford to buy clothes ready-made, you may have access to a sewing machine on which you can learn to make things. We have known both men and women who have become skilled tailors after retirement. Also, hints to younger family members may supply them with the welcome idea of gifts of clothing to you on Christmas and birthdays.

Just as or more important is keeping clothing clean, in good repair and altered to fit you if your size has changed. Older people tend gradually to get smaller in stature and lighter in weight. A favorite ten-year-old suit or dress which is still in style may be too large and need alteration; take a good hard look at it in the mirror from time to time.

Physical problems may require special clothing. Varicose veins in the legs are easily concealed and supported with trousers and special support socks for men. Women can use support hose which look attractive and now come in many colors.

A well-fitting bra becomes more important as women grow older and need more breast support. This is especially true for women with large breasts. Girdles can help to enhance certain clothing, but if you maintain a well-exercised and trim body, a girdle is likely to be unnecessary.

One last bit of advice: Don't try to dress like the young. You are the age you are; accept it matter-of-factly. Dress with style, taste and dignity, and others will respect your sense of self-esteem.

6

Learning New Patterns of Love-making

If you have been thinking about some aspects of your sex life that you would like to alter, now is the time to do it. Don't believe people who tell you that as you grow older you cannot help becoming too fixed in your ways to change. If yours was the kind of temperament interested in learning and changing earlier, it is likely to remain so all your life. Scientific studies have proved beyond question that older people can learn as well as and in some cases better than the young.

But do not underestimate the strength of habit, which is all the more powerful for being unconscious: Love-making patterns tend to become fixed and uninspired over

147

the years, often because you have not taken the time nor thought it necessary to examine them. Do you always make love at the same time of day and in the same manner? Are you excited and interested in your love life? Do your partner and you know how to please each other? It may be time to loosen up, try something new and learn to relish once again the special warmth and intimacy that are possible through love and sex.

THE SETTING FOR SEX

Look at your bedroom with a critical eye. Is it comfortable and pleasant? Is it a good place for sex? A firm comfortable bed for two is standard equipment unless illness, sleeping problems or personal preference lead you to choose single beds. The best arrangement in this case is one double bed for making love, talking and other intimacies, with a single bed in the same room or another room when you are ready to separate for sleep. A double bed encourages the closeness and sharing that enrich a couple's sense of togetherness.

Many older people develop the habit of lining up their medications on their bed stands. This is aesthetically unattractive, and a dangerous practice as well. Persons in a drowsy condition may fail to read labels, take the wrong pills in the middle of the night or accidentally take too many. We recommend that all medications be placed out of sight at a walking distance from the bed unless they are absolutely essential for emergencies (for example, nitroglycerin for persons with heart problems). In addition to protecting yourself, you will not be continually confronting yourself and your partner with reminders of your pains or infirmities.

Another thing that has struck us about many older persons' bedrooms is the gallery of family pictures of children, grandchildren, nephews, nieces and ancestors that often line the walls. This is fine for the couple married for many years, who feel comfortable in this setting. But it can be unnerving, to say the least, to the new partner who settles down expectantly in the bed and finds the other partner's relatives looking down on the proceedings.

Be sensitive to your new partner's feelings. If family pictures are interfering with your love life, banish them to another room.

Bed, of course, is a fine place for enjoyable entertainment and relaxation as well as for sex and sleep. Reading, listening to music, watching TV, eating snacks, talking over the events of the day, and massaging each other are some of the possible pleasures. Back rests or a number of large firm pillows make reading in bed more comfortable. You may want a couple of smaller pillows for sleeping. A good reading light prevents eye strain. Use nonslip rugs on the floor if you do not have carpeting. A dual-control electric blanket is quite inexpensive and useful in colder climates since the body temperatures of older people may be somewhat lower, particularly in their legs, feet and hands, and these feel cold because of slower blood circulation. But you do have to be careful with an electric blanket because it can cause drying and itching of the skin. Use it primarily to warm up the bed and your own body when you first get into bed; then turn it off. Good room ventilation is important to sound sleep. Preferably there should be air conditioning in hot climates and humidifiers in cold, dry climates if you can afford them. It is easier on the heart and circulatory system to maintain proper temperature and humidity. Finally, a phone within easy reach of the bed gives quick access to help if an emergency arises, and it is pleasant for those persons without partners who might like to call a friend and chat at bedtime.

THE TIME FOR SEX

Sex exclusively at bedtime is an easy habit to get into over the years, when daytime privacy is hard to come by and the pressures of work and family crowd your days. Yet this may not really be your favorite time. As you grow older, it may not be your most energetic period either.

Fortunately, retired people can make love any time they choose. They can stay up half the night and sleep the next day if they want to. One couple told us they often wake each other up at two or three in the morning, spend an hour or more talking and making love, then fall asleep again. Sex in the morning is a favorite time for many older people because they are rested and relaxed. Some men report greater sexual potency after a good night's sleep. Naps during the day can make for greater vigor in the evening for those who prefer nighttime love-making out of choice rather than by default. Afternoon naps themselves can be combined with making love. The flexibility made possible by retirement can allow each person to find the best time and avoid the problems of making love when one is tired, rushed, emotionally upset or not in the mood.

For those of you who are not retired we recommend experimenting with new times on weekends, holidays and vacations. When vacations away from home are not possible, take a vacation at home. If you have the house to yourself, take the phone off the hook and pretend you're not there. Make love in new locations; it need not always be in the bedroom or on the bed. Loosen up and discover what you like best.

HOW TO RELAX

A warm bath or shower before sex can relax you in a pleasant manner. Exchanging massages with your partner, turning the lights low and listening to music can also help you unwind. A *small* glass of an alcoholic beverage can be a tension reliever — we recommend dry white wine or warm Japanese sake. Warm milk, although not the world's sexiest drink, can bring relaxation. Try going to bed nude if you have never done so. If you feel more comfortable with clothes on, however, remember that it is not sexually exhilarating to your partner if you appear for bed in undershirt and boxer shorts (men) or your frayed favorite nightgown (women).

WHAT YOU CAN DO
FOR YOUR PARTNER

We are not going to describe the extensive technical knowledge which people can acquire about how to make love. This has been described adequately in other books (see appendix for examples), and in our opinion the technology of sex has been overemphasized, giving love-making more the character of a gymnastic workout or hard labor than the expression of love. This is not to say that through reading and other methods you cannot learn much that is valuable; but always remember that though skill can enhance genuine feelings of warmth and affection, it can never substitute for them or take primacy.

We do want to direct your attention to information that is especially relevant to older people. For older women, the most common sexual problem is the inability to achieve orgasm. "Frigidity" is the word often used to describe this situation, and it is an unfortunate term because it implies coldness and sexual indifference. This does not adequately explain what happens to many women.

There are periods in the sexual lives of most women when they do not experience orgasm, but this is usually transient. Temporary loss of response can have many causes, among them tiredness, emotional upset, boredom, vaginal infections or other physical ailments, drugs, lack of adequate stimulation of the clitoris. In addition, numbers of women never attain orgasm through intercourse, but can reach it through other means, such as petting, self-stimulation or oral stimulation by their partner. Orgasm by any of these means can be enjoyable. Others do not have orgasms through any method, including masturbation. Severe or total lack of sexual response on an ongoing basis can usually be traced to emotional attitudes developed during the early years of life. For some women this is extremely troubling; for others mildly so; and the remainder do not consider it to be a problem.

A good many older women have never experienced orgasm because love-making has been too quick and mechanical. When this happens, the couple needs to slow down and learn what the woman finds pleasurable and exciting. Many older men do not understand the importance of learning to stimulate the clitoral area in women, whether by hand, mouth or the penis itself.

Some older women have problems of lubrication, and it may require longer periods of sex play before lubrication actually begins. K-Y jelly can be placed in the vagina if lubrication is insufficient.

Women can learn to be sensitive and helpful when men are having problems with impotence. Try a new coital position by bending your knees and placing a pillow under your hips to elevate your pelvis, in order to more easily accommodate your partner's partially erect penis. Remember that erection can be stimulated by touching the penis, so learn to massage it. Do not pull it up toward the abdomen, where it will lose blood. Instead, push down, with pressure at the base of the penis, which will put pressure on major blood vessels to hold the blood that the penis already contains.

A woman can further the strength of an erection by literally stuffing the partially erect penis in her vagina and flexing her vaginal muscles until it achieves full erection. Many women like to hold the penis in their vagina after love-making. If they have developed their vaginal muscles, this may be possible even if the penis begins to become limp, as happens more quickly after orgasm as men grow older.

Finally, we want to stress again that a woman need not feel obligated to "give a man an ejaculation" every time they make love. Leave this up to the man to decide and concentrate on mutually enjoying the physical and emotional contact, as well as your own orgasm if it occurs.

Men and women can learn to accommodate each other's needs in other ways. If one of you is obese or has a protruding abdomen, for example, you will need to experiment to find a sexual position that allows the penis to reach the vagina. (Naturally, you should also be dieting!) The triangle technique can be used, in which the woman lies on her back with legs apart and knees sharply bent, while the man places himself over her with his hips under the angle formed by her raised knees. Another accessible position is for the man to lie on his back while the woman sits astride him.

Today older people experiment more with various sexual positions, just as do the young. There are many alternatives to the standard "missionary" position of the woman underneath, on her back, and the man on top. The most common ones are lying side by side; the woman on top; or the man entering the woman from the rear.

There are also a number of satisfying sexual alternatives to intercourse. These include mutual stimulation of each other's genitals by hand as well as stimulation of other erotic areas of the body — the mouth, neck, ears, breasts and buttocks. Oral-genital sex has come to be accepted as a common and pleasurable form of sexual activity when the usual hygienic practice of washing the genitals thoroughly beforehand is carried out. Some couples use these techniques as foreplay before intercourse. Others use them as substitutes, either because intercourse is not possible or because they prefer them.

Sex gadgets are generally a waste of money except for battery-driven vibrators, which many people find stimulating, and certain prosthetic devices which can help a man maintain a rigid penis or which can substitute completely for one. Older women should avoid douching after sex with perfumed douches or using vaginal sprays now widely sold. They are unnecessary and can cause medical problems.

SOLO SEX

Self-stimulation, or masturbation, is a common and healthy practice in later life. It provides a sexual outlet for people who do not have partners — unmarried, widowed or divorced persons — as well as for husbands or wives whose partners are ill or away. Some people use masturbation in addition to sexual intercourse, particularly if they need sex more frequently than their partner or enjoy the variety it affords. Women may experience more intense orgasms through masturbation than during intercourse.

Masturbation usually begins in childhood. It is natural for all children to explore their bodies, and most children masturbate unless they are prevented from doing it by adults. There is evidence that self-stimulation is an important preliminary to adult sexuality, enabling people to learn to recognize and satisfy their sexual feelings. The Kinsey studies of 1948 - 50 found that 92 percent of men and 62 percent of women had masturbated at some time in their life, and indications are that masturbation is increasing in women. Masturbation can continue until very late in life, and has been reported by some men in their nineties. Some people begin to masturbate for the first time after they grow older, particularly if they have no partner or become too physically incapacitated for intercourse.

It is important to free yourself of the notion that self-stimulation is unhealthy, immoral or immature. It is a source of pleasure to be learned and enjoyed for its own sake. It resolves sexual tensions, keeps sexual desire alive, is good physical exercise, and helps to preserve sexual functioning in both men and women who have no other outlets. Total abstinence from sexual activity can be tension-producing, and may result in impotence in men and loss of lubrication as well as vaginal shape in women. Vibrators can be useful aids in masturbation. Many people have sexual fantasies which add to the pleasure of self-stimulation.

COMMUNICATING WITH YOUR PARTNER ABOUT SEX

Have you ever freely talked to your partner about sex? About what stimulates you the most? Do you feel embarrassed or too awkward to ask? Has your partner ever candidly asked you? Many couples assume that one doesn't have to talk, since sex "comes naturally." This is not so. We are all different from one another and we need to express our likes and dislikes rather than merely hope our partners can read our minds or know intuitively how to please us.

Begin by discussing your feelings about talking about sex itself. Then help each other by telling your partner what gives you pleasure. Finally, try in every way possible to do what is pleasurable for each other. You may be surprised at what you don't know about your partner and what you may have been reluctant to admit about yourself. Learn the art of sexual give and take, where you give joyfully and generously to the other person in the expectation that he or she will do the same

161

for you. Some couples share their sexual fantasies with each other. You can also reminisce, talking about your first memories of sex, your early sexual attitudes and those of your family, and perhaps your feelings about what it means to be a man or a woman. Compare notes on what you would most like to change about yourself and about your partner sexually. Be thoughtful and kind about the way you express any dissatisfactions you may feel. Do not hesitate to express your warmth and affection when these are honestly felt.

Sex and marriage manuals can help couples learn more about themselves and each other. Many of you may be familiar with T. H. Van de Velde's *Ideal Marriage,* first published in 1930 and now in its forty-fifth printing. A veritable explosion of books has appeared since then. You will find it useful to take a fresh look from time to time at what you know about sexuality, and at the current attitudes of society toward sex. People themselves change over the years. What might have been stimulating to you ten years ago may interest you much less now, and you may develop new sexual interests which did not exist previously. Thus it is important to keep aware of your own growth and change, and to continue to learn about sexuality. We have recommended several books in the appendix. We would like to see teaching films and tapes become available which are specifically addressed to medical and other problems that can affect sexuality in later life.*

*Films and tapes are beginning to appear for other special groups, such as those with spinal cord injuries.

7

People Without Partners

As they grow older many people find themselves without partners. This is especially true of women. In 1970 more than half of all women over sixty were widows, as compared to about 15 percent of men. Another 5 percent of men and 7 percent of women this age had never married, and about 2 percent were divorced. Finding yourself alone is a fact of late life that increases with time.

Obviously there are differences between the life styles of those who never married and who over the years have created a circle of friends and intimates that substituted for an immediate family, and those who are abruptly separated from a spouse by death or divorce and now find themselves on their own, for the first time in many years or possibly in their lives. Where the widowed person is deprived of both the shared intimacies and the interdependence of long marriage and the social patterns that go with being a couple, the single or long-divorced man or woman is accustomed to living on his or her own. Still, as one grows older, time and deaths erode the circle of relatives and close friends regardless of marital status, and some people find an increasing emptiness in the later years that needs to be filled. You cannot depend on the healing power of time alone to ease grief or loss, or to alleviate loneliness. New relationships will not simply happen. You will have to take an active part in putting your life together again.

Where Do You Start? Initiative is the first requisite. It is up to you to take charge of your life, to decide what you want and what you should do about it. This does not mean you must deliberately be "on the hunt" for a possible partner — unless such forthrightness is natural to you. You may want no more than opportunities to meet people who are congenial and likely to share your own interests, and the way to do this is to look for activities that support these interests. You will feel less tense and pressured if you are doing what you like to do. A sense of pleasure and purpose in what you are doing will encourage you to enjoy, learn, give of yourself and make friends.

Some People Worry about Etiquette.   If you are not certain, follow the golden rule and your own common sense. Many older people are still bound by the customs they were taught as youngsters and many of these formalities make no sense today. Women used to be told it was improper to call a man. But if you are interested, you do not have to wait for invitations from a man; simply behave as you do when you want to get in touch with a friend. He has the option of accepting or refusing just as you do when a man (or woman) calls you. If he accepts your invitation, a friendship or a relationship may develop or it may not — but you will have taken a perfectly appropriate and dignified initiative that allows you an *active* role in finding new friends and activities.

Building a Social Life. A variety of activities is available to older people without partners who want to develop a fuller social life. One of the best opportunities of all is through your work, if you have not yet retired or if you are offered the chance to return to work, on a full or part-time basis, after retirement. For many people, work is a major factor in self-esteem. If you do not have a job but are interested and able, consider the possibility of looking actively for part-time work, both for the rewards of being useful and for the opportunities it offers to meet new people under daily and unself-conscious circumstances.

Where one lives will affect the number of choices one has for activities that will widen one's social circle, but except in quite isolated rural communities there are more possibilities than you may realize. If you are politically minded, for example,

167

you can volunteer your help at your local political club. Voluntary work for worthwhile causes, social service agencies, nearby hospitals or schools may provide you with rewarding work, at the same time that it brings you into contact with other people who share similar concerns. Those who like to be active and out of doors can seek out health clubs, hiking and biking clubs, wilderness, nature and birdwatching groups. Any special interests can lead to social contacts.

If you can't find something that fits your particular taste, consider organizing it yourself. Musicians can start amateur chamber music groups or orchestras, or jazz, western, country and ethnic music groups. Many towns and cities have amateur choirs, where an interest in singing is the only prerequisite. Painting, theater, handicraft and folk art clubs are popular; if there is a Y in your community, you may find it is already sponsoring such activities. We know one Midwestern woman who started a sewing circle that attracted men who wanted to learn to quilt and do needlepoint. Organizing potluck dinners is a good way to cut costs and promote sociability. Cooking clubs attract more women than men, but cooking is becoming a male avocation as well. Woodworking and carpentry, wine making and tasting, chess and investment clubs attract many older men and a number of women. Bridge clubs are popular.

If you live in a city or its suburbs, you have the advantage of a wider choice of activities. Senior centers and community centers offer recreational opportunities for older persons; there are now over five thousand senior centers and clubs in the United States, operated by churches, synagogues, social clubs and nonprofit corporations.* These centers offer shows, parties, music, beauty salons, handicrafts,

*A listing by states can be found in the *Directory of Senior Centers and Clubs — National Resource,* published in 1974 by the National Council on the Aging, Inc., 1828 L Street, N.W., Washington, D.C. 20036. This publication costs $10. Your congressmen and senators have copies, so you can write and ask them to direct you to centers and clubs near you. If this fails, write directly to the National Council on the Aging.

trips, discussion groups and a variety of other things to do at the same time that you are encountering new people. Religious activities are another important way of meeting people. Many churches and synagogues sponsor singles clubs, and some are beginning to expand these to fit the needs of older members. Talk to your clergyman about starting such a group if one does not exist in your locale.

If you live in a rural area or a small town, you are more likely to know everyone who might be available as a friend or a companion in your area, just as they, in turn, know you. For variety you may want to make and visit friends in neighboring communities and get to larger urban areas for activities whenever possible. Trips and vacations away from home can be a way of making new acquaintances. If you don't have a car, arrange to share rides with others if you can. Neighbors and friends may be willing to serve as a taxi for you. (You may feel freer in asking them if you offer a modest fee.) Certain rural areas and many small towns are connected by bus lines.

A small but growing number of older people have begun to live together in communal settings as a means of increasing their social contacts, cutting costs and sharing housekeeping duties. Some communes are made up only of older people, while others include people of all ages. Most of these are in large houses, though we have also heard of large apartments that are occupied communally and free of the chores of caring for a house and yard.

The two major organizations for older people, the National Council of Senior Citizens (national office at 1911 K Street, N.W., Room 202, Washington, D.C. 20006) and the American Association of Retired Persons — National Retired Teachers Association (national office at 1909 K Street N.W., Washington, D.C. 20006), may have chapters in your area where meetings of many kinds take place. Look in your phone book, or, if necessary, check with their national offices to see if there is a chapter near you. Five to six million older people belong to one or both of these organizations, which provide significant political advocacy and services (such as discount drugs, insurance coverage supplemental to Medicare, low-cost travel, etc.) as well as social opportunities.

If you would like to combine opportunities for meeting people with social and political activism, the Gray Panthers (6342 Greene Street, Philadelphia, Pa. 19144), an organization which works vigorously on behalf of the older population, is adding local chapters rapidly and includes younger as well as older people in its membership. The National Caucus on the Black Aged (1730 M Street, N.W., Suite 811, Washington, D.C. 20036) focuses on the problems of older black people. Many older men and women also participate in local, state and national politics, meeting a wide variety of people at the same time that they give useful service.

If you are the parent of a child or adolescent, Parents Without Partners clubs can be a source of contacts and of help to you, both as a parent and as a single person.*

Ocean cruises can be good fun and some

people do meet partners this way, though they generally attract many more women than men and they are expensive. If you have the money, are interested in where you are going and like to travel, you can enjoy yourself and make friends on a cruise. Don't be afraid to ask the ship's purser for help in meeting others and seating you with compatible dining companions. Younger men who are attracted to older women may use cruises as a meeting place, but be careful that they aren't interested chiefly in your money.

A more inexpensive way to travel sociably is to go on bus tours, some of which cover the entire United States and parts of Canada. You can get a ticket for use nationwide at reasonable rates. Take a friend, go by yourself or with a group, and be open to meeting new people along the way.

Dance lessons are widely touted for older

---

*Recently widowed older people have been finding support and direction for their lives through the Widow to Widow program, which originated in Boston and is now being tested in other cities by the American Association of Retired Persons.

people, but be wary because the commercial ones can be greatly overpriced and sometimes fraudulent, offering "lifetime contracts" and noncancelable contracts. If you can't locate a reputable and reasonably priced place to learn, find friends who will teach you. If you are a good dancer, offer to teach someone else. Square dancing, folk and ballroom dancing may bring back memories (as well as the dance steps themselves) from your past. A number of cities have relatively inexpensive public ballrooms; Roseland Dance City in New York, for example, has special matinees for older people. Friendships and romances can begin in such settings — Roseland has a plaque on its wall engraved with the names of married couples who first met there.

High school, college and other reunions offer men and women the chance to renew acquaintance with compatible people whom they knew earlier in life and who are now widowed or divorced themselves. We have known childhood sweethearts who met again and married after each had raised families and then was widowed.

Family reunions and family contacts in general are another way to get in touch with people who may be seeking new relationships; there is a long and honorable tradition, for example, of widows and widowers who are in-laws developing close relationships that end not infrequently in marriage.

Commercial singles clubs and computer dating services are not very receptive to older persons. This is just as well since they can be an expensive and uncomfortable way to meet people. It is preferable to organize your own singles club in your church or synagogue or social organization.

Occasionally older people advertise in the newspapers for companions. This is admittedly risky, though sometimes it works out well; often, however, one can be bitterly disappointed, misled and even exploited. If you want to try, be wary.

If you are simply looking for an escort or temporary companion for a business or social event, there are legitimate agencies which will provide people, for a fee. Some escort services, however, are fronts for hiring sex partners (both male and female).

If you are uneasy about commercial escort services, call your local clergyman to ask whether he knows someone who could accompany you, or get in touch with a local older-persons group or senior center.

Don't overlook born matchmakers among your friends, acquaintances, colleagues, your children or other family members. Some people have highly developed sensibilities and can be very helpful in finding men or women you would enjoy meeting. But do save yourself time and trouble by picking your matchmakers carefully; look for someone whose judgment you respect and who knows you well.

Can You Be Exploited?   It is possible. It may not happen often, but it is up to you to know what to look out for and how to protect yourself. Exploitation occurs in an emotional relationship when someone "uses" someone else without giving much in return. Some older men (and far more rarely, women) will marry primarily to gain a housekeeper or nurse. The "romance" disappears as soon as the marriage vows are exchanged, and the woman discovers she has been recruited primarily to perform services. It is much wiser, of course, to take time to learn as much as you can about the other person before you decide to marry. The history of his or her relationships with the opposite sex can be illuminating. Most exploiters have a long history of taking advantage of others.

At other times the exploiter may be after your money or property. Matrimonial swindles through lonely-hearts clubs and correspondence with people you have never met who claim a romantic interest in you are notorious. The tip-off comes when the person begins to be inordinately interested in your property, your money or your will. If you suspect this is happening to you, get to a lawyer, clergyman or someone else you can trust, and ask him to advise you.

Older men and women may be exploited more directly by younger people who pretend a romantic involvement. Look out for persons who suddenly "fall in love" with you after they discover you have money or property. Even people on a modest pension can be taken advantage of by those who are too dependent or unmotivated to work for themselves, and are looking for someone to take care of them financially.

Qualities That Foster New Relationships. It will help you in your first ventures into meeting new people if you remember that the men and women you encounter are as likely to be feeling tentative or somewhat shy as you are. Actually, you will find that what you look for in other people — as companions, as friends, as co-workers or as intimates — are qualities they seek just as eagerly in you. Warmth and sensitivity to other people's feelings are greatly valued. One can be quiet or lively, according to one's temperament, as long as curiosity and an active mind underlie this temperament. Imagination, responsiveness, a sense of humor are welcomed.

Certain personal qualities foster the art of companionship. Most people respond to a sense of vitality and energy. People who are pleasantly assertive (not domineering) have a greater chance of meeting new people and forming rewarding relationships, simply because they do not leave all the initiative up to others.

Qualities That Hinder New Relationships. It is important that you maintain a positive approach that transcends or tempers any problems you have. We know from our clinical experience that certain personality features can act as barriers to new relationships. Many older people have had much to endure in the way of the deaths of spouses or of friends, of difficulties with children, of financial burdens and loneliness and an increasing feeling of uselessness. Under these pressures, it is not uncommon for one to feel that life has been unfair, to bear a grudge against one's circumstances. But this resentment is likely to make other people wary of becoming involved with you. It is depressing to be with someone who is always complaining or petulant, and whose outlook is pessimistic. It takes a deliberate, conscious act of will to overcome the grim dependency on all that seems sour in one's life; but unless this is done, the chances for new and enriching

179

relationships are diminished.

Special Problems for Women.
Unattached older women, especially those who are widowed or divorced, often find themselves squeezed out of activities that involve couples. Hostesses at dinner parties feel they must have a man available for each woman guest, couples coming two-by-two like the creatures on Noah's Ark. Though she may not acknowledge this, the hostess may also find the presence of a widow or divorcee an uncomfortable reminder of the possibility that she may not have her husband with her forever, and may even think it possible her guest will set her cap for him.

If you are frequently left out socially, one solution is to join with other single people and organize your own parties and activities. Develop a circle of friends in which friendship rather than gender is the key to getting together, and make these times occasions where people of any age or marital status and either sex can enjoy one another's company. Your married friends can also be invited, so that they get used to the idea that there is more than one way to share social events.

If you are a divorced woman, be prepared to have some people see *you* as a failure; they make the conscious or unconscious assumption that the breakup of your marriage was caused by a flaw in you. Talk this over with understanding people who care about you. If you do indeed have problems, you may want to seek professional help.

Both widows and divorcees find that some men (married or otherwise) assume that women who are sexually experienced are automatically available and willing. Indeed, these men may see themselves as doing you a sexual favor. If this annoys or upsets you, simply tell them so.

Special Problems for Men. As a general rule, unattached men have fewer *social* difficulties. Even those who had not thought themselves socially very accomplished when they were younger may be surprised to find how eagerly accepted and actively pursued they now are. This is largely because there are fewer men than women; and a man who enjoys relationships with women is likely to have ample opportunity for them. On the other hand, if you are a man who finds it annoying or troubling to be treated like a commodity in short supply, you will have to make this clear, or else remove yourself from those situations where this tends to occur.

Uncertainty can be a problem for men. Many men, like many women, are hesitant, shy or dubious about their ability to handle personal relationships. To find yourself valued as an available man as you grow older is not automatically reassuring if your inner self doubts its sophistication, skill or appeal to the opposite sex. Most men have been conditioned to believe that anything short of confident "masculinity" is shameful, a failure of their maleness. Though a woman may have similar problems of self-confidence, society has not pressured her into feeling "unwomanly" as a result. Any man troubled by doubts about his skill in social and sexual situations should know that he has plenty of company, and that this is no reflection on his manliness. He should also remember that most women he meets are not going to measure him against some impossible ideal and judge him a failure. Further, the man who is shy, diffident or uncertain about his competence will have to make the same effort of will, and exercise the same degree of initiative, that a hesitant woman must undertake. Without this determination relationships will not just happen for him any more than for her.

When a man doubts his sexual performance, or fears that the woman with whom he is making love may be measuring him against the behavior of a previous partner, it *will* affect his sexual ability. It takes an active effort on both their parts to make the present moment satisfying to each of them. Memories of past love-making should not be allowed to dominate the present. Now is what matters. What each of you can give the other should concern you more than anything else. A caring woman who offers love and reassurance to a man who is feeling uncertain about his skill will restore his confidence. Sexual problems with deep roots may require professional help, but the self-doubt that has its roots in shyness and uneasiness about performance — which is much more common — is often alleviated by thoughtfulness and tenderness.

Handling Refusals, Rebuffs and Disappointments. However confident they may appear on the surface, a great many men and women worry about rebuffs when they initiate or respond to a social opportunity. How can you handle refusals and disappointments? It is natural to feel hurt, but you should not let this feeling persist. You have to accept the possibility of rejection whenever you involve yourself with others, so be matter-of-fact about it. It is, after all, the other person's right — as it is yours when you are approached. It should not deter you from further involvements. Remember that rejection can also be useful, by keeping people apart who would be unhappy together.

Obviously, there will be some occasions when the rebuff is rude and takes no account of your feelings. Inevitably, a certain proportion of your social contacts will prove to be unpleasant, and sometimes even painful. This is unavoidable in human relationships at any age. The point to remember is that refusals or disappointments do not mean you are a failure as a person. If you are losing confidence and feel you need a fresh perspective on yourself, talk over your experiences with a close friend. Then try again. Draw on the experience you have gained even from the unpleasant event. Take a few chances. Above all, do not waste time berating yourself for what does not work out. Learn to assess wisely the difference between what is your responsibility and that which is beyond your control.

Moving Too Fast. What if one partner in a newly acquainted couple moves too quickly toward intimacy? Many older people dread the thought of the widow who is husband-hunting or the man who is on the make sexually on the first date. Once again, use your common sense. Don't be afraid to tell the other person if you are feeling pushed. Be sensitive to your companion's feelings, especially if you yourself are an impulsive or action-oriented individual. A relationship that is going to be more than merely temporary needs time to build. People must explore each other's feelings and learn more about each other. Decide together what pace to set. Many people are not ready for physical intimacies — much less marriage — until they feel a mutual understanding and affection. An enduring partnership is based on thoughtfulness as well as attraction.

Should I Remarry? This question tends to be asked by men and women whose previous marriages have been unhappy or difficult. They assume second marriages are doomed to repeat the same mistakes. Obviously, all marriages have problems and the partners must work to solve them. But a second marriage is not likely to be any more problem-ridden than the first one, and because people do change, and do learn from life, there is a very good chance of a better choice of mate and of a better all-around adjustment the second time.

Occasionally men and women worry

about whether they have grown too old to remarry. If you care deeply for someone and want to marry again, by all means do so. There have been many happy marriages that began at sixty, or seventy, or even later. The reasons why one marries have far more effect on the success of the marriage than the age or past histories of the partners. Those who marry for love or companionship are likelier to live together happily than those who are seeking a place to live, or financial gain, or a housekeeper or nurse. Men and women who have known each other for some time, or who have shared work or other common interests, may have a sturdier base on which to build their life together.

Freeing Yourself from the Past. It is often very difficult for the man or woman who has been widowed to look ahead to a new partner without feelings of guilt or disloyalty to the memory of the dead spouse. Once the period of mourning is over and the initial shock and grief have abated, however, you owe it to yourself to become realistic about your right to a life of your own. This means the appropriate preservation of your memories, but no excessive dwelling in the past. Enshrinement of the past — its furnishings, tokens, memories — can signify a rejection of living. It may be necessary to put away some of its more obvious symbols, such as your wedding ring. It is not a betrayal of your past marriage to accept the present and build a future.

Affairs in Later Life. Many couples who come to care for each other want to marry because marriage confirms for them the permanence and depth of their commitment. For some older people, in addition, the idea of living together without marriage goes against moral or religious scruples. Couples have the right to decide for themselves, however, whether they wish to legalize their partnership by marriage. It is possible for sincere and caring relationships to exist without marriage if the older man and woman elect to live this way. The decision may involve deliberate choice, or may be the result of necessity. Two people can care deeply for each other and want to live together, but feel that marriage would set limits on an independence they have come to value. We have known older men and women who nursed spouses through long chronic illness until death, and who felt that they did not want to enter into another marriage that might put them through the same ordeal again.

There are also instances in which marriage is not possible. Everyone knows of unhappy marriages which continue for years because one spouse will not agree to divorce, forcing the other to seek a partner outside marriage. In other marriages, one member may have been incapacitated or chronically ill for a long time, leaving the other without a satisfying sexual and emotional outlet. (Affairs are more likely if the marital couple had an unsatisfying emotional relationship to begin with, or if one partner is mentally impaired or institutionalized.) Sometimes the children of a widowed parent object so strongly to his or her remarriage that an affair is the only recourse.

Economic factors enter into more

decisions not to remarry than many people realize. When income is limited, the fact that Social Security laws penalize widows for remarrying by forcing them to give up their survivors' benefits keeps many of them from new marriages. Recent legislation has improved this situation somewhat, but penalties still remain. Meanwhile thousands of older men and women live with each other outside of marriage in what the Miami *Herald* has called "Social Security sin" in order to preserve their pensions. Medicaid benefits can also be a barrier to remarriage. If one partner has been receiving Medicaid, marriage would mean suspending that support until the entire savings of the new spouse were used up; only then could Medicaid be resumed. Indeed, there have been cases where husband and wife divorced each other, though continuing to live together, in order for one of them to be eligible for Medicaid.

Homosexual unions exist among older people, but little is known about them. Few older homosexual couples have "come out" and revealed their relationship openly, preferring to present themselves as roommates or friends. Homosexuality was not considered an acceptable personal choice when they were younger and they would have been subjected to social censure. Fortunately, this climate is changing. It is our impression that many more older people have chosen homosexuality as a way of life than is commonly realized.

Older people who are considering an affair, or have guilt feelings about being involved in one, will sometimes call upon clergymen or counselors for advice. It can be a difficult situation for a clergyman to resolve if his theological views come into conflict with his humanity and compassion for the individual couple. One minister described a couple in their seventies who approached him with embarrassment and guilt because they wanted their union acknowledged by the church. They had been living together for a number of years, barely subsisting on their incomes and financially unable to marry. The minister decided to "bless" their cohabitation with a simple ceremony that had no religious or legal authority but left them relieved and renewed in their faith.

Living with Your Children. Living with your children, as roughly 20 percent of older people do, can put a damper on your social life unless you take steps to prevent it. Don't depend on your children to recognize your needs for privacy. You will have to take the initiative, and discuss this with them frankly. Work out ways of sharing the space available in the home, so that there will be times when you can entertain people privately. Some houses are large enough for you to have your own suite of rooms, which makes a separate social life easier. But most older people will have a bedroom at most, and sometimes even this will have to be shared with another member of the family. If you have your own room and it is a reasonable size, you can furnish it as a combination bedroom — sitting room and entertain your friends there. If small children live in the house, a lock or latch on the door will keep them from running in and out until they learn to knock and enter only on invitation. Your bed can be a couch by day, and you should also have a comfortable chair, a small table or trays for eating, a TV set, radio or phonograph, pleasant lighting and other amenities for entertaining. If you must share a bedroom, arrange to have sole use of the room at certain times. There may be difficulties in entertaining privately in the family living or dining room unless you and your family have worked out a practical schedule. It is easier if there is also a recreation room or den. If your resources permit, you might want to help finance the construction of additional space or undertake some remodeling.

Make your children aware of your desire for privacy before you move in with them. When it is they who are moving in with you, things are usually a bit easier because you are on your own territory to begin with. The crucial element in living successfully with one's children is to be able to talk openly with them about problems and cooperate in solving them.

Sexual Life in Institutions. The 5 percent of persons over sixty-five who live in homes for the aging, nursing homes, chronic-disease hospitals and other long-term-care institutions have a very painful problem. In general they are denied the opportunity for any private social and sexual life of their own. Visitors are in full view of roommates and staff and can be overheard by them. Most people in institutions are widowed, and a few are divorced or single. But even those who have marital partners are seldom able to share conjugal visits, where the patient is provided a private time and place with his or her spouse. One older man described how he locked himself and his wife in a bathroom on one of her visits so that they could make love. There was no other place to get away from the other patients and the nursing staff.

Intimacies of any kind between unmarried patients, even hugging or kissing or holding hands, are frowned on despite the fact that they are consenting adults. Even persons who, understandably, resort to masturbation because they have no other sexual outlet run the risk of being discovered and reprimanded like children.

We realize that most older persons caught in these situations are reluctant to complain to the management. We urge you to do so, however, since this is a serious infringement of your rights as an adult. Ask the administrator of your particular institution to provide whatever privacy you and other patients should have. If you need outside support, ask your relatives, friends, clergyman, doctor or lawyer to help you in stating your cause. Speak to other patients who have a similar complaint and make it a joint project. You can also alert groups who are interested in the problems of older persons, such as local chapters of the Gray Panthers, the American Association of Retired Persons and the National Council of Senior Citizens.* New federal regulations provide some right to privacy, but only for married couples, and only

*If you have difficulty finding a local chapter of these organizations, write to their national offices:

Gray Panthers: 6342 Greene Street, Philadelphia, Pa. 19144

in those nursing homes that participate in federal Medicare and Medicaid programs (more than two-thirds do not). These regulations are not being uniformly enforced, and failure to observe them is ground for legal action.

American Association of Retired Persons: 1909 K Street, N.W., Washington D.C. 20006

National Council of Senior Citizens: 1911 K Street, N.W., Room 202, Washington, D.C. 20005

8

Dating, Remarriage and Your Children

Our patient files contain many examples of conflicts between parents and their adult children that develop when a parent is widowed (or divorced) and attempts to build a new life through dating and, possibly, remarriage:

"My daughter doesn't like my fiancée, and thinks she is only interested in my money."

"My son Jim feels I'd be a fool to marry Harry, that Harry has always been a run-around."

"My children think I'm crazy to want

197

a man. I wouldn't dare tell them what I did on my cruise to Jamaica.''

Not all children create problems. Many are pleased at the thought of their parents leading full and satisfying lives. Others have realistic worries about practical implications; they may welcome the remarriage of a father to a somewhat younger woman, because she will be able to nurse him as he grows older, but may feel threatened if their mother marries an older man, because it will be a burden on her and potentially on them if he falls ill.

For still other children the reactions are entirely emotional. The thought of a parent becoming involved with a new partner can provoke anxiety, threat, jealousy, hurt, anger or grief. They may be strongly inclined to offer unasked-for advice and even to take over if they feel a parent is making a mistake. Coercion, threats and angry withdrawal are not uncommon.

There are numerous reasons why adult children react so negatively. Those who never became fully independent psychologically of a parent will use that parent to fulfill emotional needs that should be met by their own mates and friends. This can be assumed if your child acts possessive or personally aggrieved when you become involved in a relationship with someone, and it is not unlike the behavior of a wounded lover. It is likely that you yourself (perhaps unconsciously) have encouraged an inappropriately close relationship with this child, or that other circumstances have kept the child from emancipating him- or herself. Age is not a factor in these situations. Your fifty-year-old child can be dependent in this way even though he or she is married and has children of his own. Under these circumstances, the best approach is to let your children know, kindly but definitely, that you intend to lead your own life, and to encourage them to do likewise.

Children will sometimes try to preserve the memory of their deceased parent (or your former relationship with a divorced spouse) by the process of *enshrinement*. They maintain a fierce reverence for the past and want to see nothing changed, so they consider any new relationships you enter into an affront to their other parent. You can then find yourself accused of being selfish, insensitive or disloyal; and if they succeed in making you feel guilty, you may be compelled to sever your new relationship. This is a mistake. Your children need to work through their own anger and grief at the death (or divorce) which ended their parents' marriage, and to complete this grief work. They are often bound to the past by a mixture of positive and negative feelings, and it is this ambivalence which must be resolved. Talk to them freely about their feelings, listen to their reactions and try honestly to answer any questions or clarify any confusion that you can. Let them know, also, how you have handled your own feelings about their other parent.

Another problem can develop if your children hold grievances and grudges against you which they demonstrate by refusing to condone your right to build a new life for yourself. Some of these grievances may be lifelong, others recent; some may be misconceptions and misunderstandings of your actions toward them, particularly during their childhood, and others may be legitimate. Adult children may become critical of their parents because their parents were always critical of them. Others remember being harshly punished or humiliated for innocent sexual experiences in childhood and grew up thinking sex was wrong or dirty, the sex lives of their parents included. If you can begin listening openly to their grievances — and it may be difficult — there is a chance that you and your children can develop a new understanding and respect for each other. Be ready to admit where you may have failed; but don't take the blame for everything. They — your children — and your former spouse played their roles too. The point is not to pin down a culprit, find a "bad guy" or allay grievances by making yourself a martyr, but to clarify what happened, why it happened and whether anything can now be done to build a better relationship. Frank talk itself sometimes heals old wounds. And when it doesn't *you* decide what choice you are going to make.

Next we must look at a problem that

can terrorize a parent — the spoiled child. This is the child who grows up believing himself or herself to be inordinately important and never stops believing it. Every spoiled child has one and usually two parents who were easily intimidated, overindulgent or lax with discipline. A favorite tactic of such a child is to threaten to withdraw love if the parent does not cater to his or her wishes. This tactic is all the more devastating when the child grows to middle age and attains greater power as the parent becomes older and loses status and authority. The sooner you get a grip on this situation, the better. Do not let your son or daughter dictate to you. It isn't good for you and it isn't good for your child. It may be frightening to think of losing this love, but remember that children rarely "divorce" their parents, at least not for long, and particularly if they know basically that you care about them. Spoiled children have an intuitive understanding of power since they learned to use it expertly at a very early age. Use power in your turn, to let them know the score.

First of all, *keep your grip on your own*

money and property. Then start making a few of your own decisions, particularly about your personal life. Get outside authority figures to help you if you need them in the initial battles that are bound to come. Your lawyer, clergyman or a respected friend or family member may be able to support you when you waver, or speak for you if at first you can't. You can be heartened by the knowledge that spoiled children usually develop respect for people who refuse to be manipulated.

Sometimes parents find that their children harbor the ignorance and misinformation about sex in later life which we have discussed in earlier chapters. They cling to the parental image of you only as Mom or Dad, and do not recognize or want to recognize that you need sex and love just as they do. It is probable that you have encouraged this yourself by playing only the parent role whenever you were around them. A good antidote is to tell them more about your social interests and to bring your friends and dates home to meet them. You can still retain your privacy, but they should become aware that you are entitled to emotional and personal commitments. Though they may never feel entirely at ease about your right to a sexually satisfying life, they can often be helped to come to terms with its reality.

Finally, we come to a most painful problem, the will-watching child — found particularly in those families where there will be an estate after a parent's death. This child is forever worrying about his or her share of your estate and casts a cold eye on anyone you may be dating or thinking of marrying. A child like this will often plant suspicions in your mind that any close friend or prospective mate is after whatever money you have. Older people can be and have been exploited, of course, but if your mind is sound, you should rely on your own judgment and perhaps that of trusted friends or advisers — and *not* on a child with a family reputation for overconcern about money or an inclination to avarice. (If you begin to have any question about your own judgment, you can seek legal advice to set up a conservatorship. This will protect you, your funds and your estate.)

What makes a child obsessive about his inheritance? Many things: parental overindulgence, feelings of being unloved, modeling after a long-standing family overemphasis on money, or lack of training in the pleasure there is in generosity and sharing with others. Simple selfishness and greed also exist. This is a difficult problem to rectify unless your child is motivated to discover the basis of his or her attitudes toward material possessions. You can try to understand any part you may have played in shaping these attitudes and see what changes in them you can make. But also protect yourself financially and emotionally from capitulating to your child's demands. Your estate is your own to disperse as you see fit. If your son or daughter puts the pressure on, it may help to keep the provisions of your will secret. If the child is capable of maintaining some rationality in this area, however, it may be helpful for him or her to know exactly what you intend to do so that he can learn to live with it. The important thing is to be decisive, and remain unintimidated by veiled or open threats, pressures and pleadings focused upon your property.

In general, your children's emotional reactions toward your personal life are likely to run deep and require your special attention if you are to avoid unnecessary alienation and hostility. Family councils and heart-to-heart talks can help enormously. But if all else fails, look for professional advice and try to get your children to join you. If they refuse, seek help by yourself, but make it clear to your children (and to yourself) that you are working toward their eventual acceptance of your new life.

PREMARITAL LEGAL PLANNING

Premarital legal planning is advisable and often essential. We will focus on only one important form of such planning, the premarital agreement or contract.* Alternative forms (trusts, for example)

---

*Also called prenuptial or antenuptial agreements — not to be confused with modern marriage contracts, which stipulate marital duties and are not legally binding. Premarital agreements deal only with money and other property.

should also be considered but are beyond the scope of this book. Whatever kind of premarital planning you elect will require the consultation of a lawyer.

There are many parents who want to leave at least part of their estate directly to their children and are concerned about the effects of remarriage on this intention. If you are planning to remarry and want to make special financial arrangements for the benefit of your children or any other persons, you and your spouse-to-be can work out a premarital agreement. In most states these agreements are a time-honored method for allaying the fears of children and planning one's estate wisely and in their best interests. Such agreements also protect older people themselves, by keeping their resources intact and unavailable to anyone but designated persons. Wealthy people have traditionally used premarital agreements for marriages at any age, in order to protect family estates. Now that people live longer, with more late-life marriages and with more extensive estates to dispose of, premarital agreements are increasingly common. The agreement customarily describes what will *not* be available to the prospective spouse. To be legally enforceable such an agreement must be in writing, by reason of the Statute of Frauds in force in all states.

How does a premarital agreement work? Let's take a couple who plan to marry, each of whom has been widowed and has children. The premarital agreement enables them to plan their respective estates in the way that suits them. The advantage to the children lies in the fact that their parent's new spouse will receive an amount less than ordinary under the Statute of Descent and Distributions and the children will receive more. An added advantage is that under such an agreement the children will receive somewhat more than if the parent had died intestate (without a will).

A premarital agreement is different from a will. It is a waiver to the right of the spouse to a certain minimum claim to your property at death. A will can be changed at any time without the spouse's knowledge or consent, while a premarital agreement can be amended only with the consent of both parties. It is binding as of the time of the marriage, whereas a will goes into effect only at the time of death. A will can of course be changed to give a spouse more and the children less than the premarital agreement stated. But unless the will stipulates this, the spouse cannot lay claim to any more than the premarital agreement provides.

People of modest means may also find premarital agreements useful even though their estates are small. An illustration might be the widower of moderate assets with children by his first wife, who had assisted him in earning the money he has accumulated and whose children contributed actively as well. Now that he wants to remarry, there is some resentment on the part of the children that the new bride will be automatically entitled to one-third (or whatever proportion is operative in a particular state) of their father's entire estate in the event of his death. If he chooses to do so, the father can decide to contract a premarital agreement which provides something less than one-third of the estate for the new wife, with the rest going to children or grandchildren. The financial gain to the children may be small, but emotionally it may mean a great deal.

There are situations where premarital agreements have been challenged, and the courts have in some cases upheld those challenges if fraud was involved or certain formalities had not been observed. The law says that the contracting parties must be in a confidential (or fiduciary) relationship to each other, meaning that there must be a good-faith disclosure of assets. For example, the failure of a man to reveal that he has several hundred thousand dollars (who tells his bride-to-be that he has only $20,000 so that she agrees to take the sum of $5,000 in the event of his death) makes the agreement subject to challenge on the basis of fraud.

Another problem is separation or divorce. Premarital agreements often provide for the eventuality of death or divorce, and these agreements are expressly recognized in about one-fourth of the states by statute and in most of the other states by judicial decision. When the agreement deals not only with the division of property in the event of death, but with the possibility of divorce as well, problems may be encountered. For example, many states hold that agreements entered into before marriage to provide for divorce payments in the event of separation are invalid.

How much should you tell your children about your premarital agreement, or the making of or changing your will? Some parents inform each child fully or have their lawyer do so. Others give a general picture but not the specifics. Still others keep everything totally secret. What you do depends on your own judgment. Children may be relieved to have at least a general idea of your intentions. But if privacy about your own financial affairs is important to you, you have every right to keep your arrangements to yourself.

Legal fees average $30 to $80 an hour. Usually one to four hours will be enough to work out premarital agreements, depending on their complexity. If resources for legal fees are limited, some parents ask their children to help with financing the making or changing of wills and premarital agreements. The rationale is that the children will be the ultimate beneficiaries of such actions. Another source of professional help in these circumstances is local legal aid societies.

9

Where to Go for Help

We have discussed those things that older people can do for themselves to understand and remedy sexual, personal and social problems. But when such problems persist, outside professional help may be a good idea.

A thorough evaluation is crucial to determining exactly where the problem lies. The first step in any evaluation of sexual problems in this age group should *always* be a medical examination. Physical problems can cause serious sexual difficulties by themselves or they can team up with emotional or social problems to create a baffling group of sexual symptoms. Unraveling the medical aspects of sexual problems may be quite simple or terribly complicated, but it cannot be neglected.

Finding a Doctor. How do you find a doctor who is knowledgeable about sex? How do you find one who is interested in older people and understands the special problems of sex in later life? Frankly, it may be difficult. Many doctors have not had sex education as part of their medical-school training. Those graduating from medical school before 1961 have had no formal training in this area. This has slowly changed, but you will still find that many doctors are surprisingly unenlightened and embarrassed to talk about sexual activity throughout the course of the life cycle. Many draw primarily upon their own personal sexual philosophy and experience. This is especially true about sex in the later years. They may also share personally the culture's negative attitude toward old age. In some public general hospitals, doctors routinely stop prescribing estrogen for women after sixty in the belief that sexual difficulties are irrelevant at that age.

Adding to the difficulty of a search for a sympathetic and knowledgeable doctor is the fact that most doctors have not had systematic training in the general medical problems of older people. This is slowly changing and some medical-school programs have begun to include geriatrics — the study of old age — in their curriculum, but lack of knowledge and interest remains widespread among practicing physicians. Two national organizations, the American Geriatrics Society (10 Columbus Circle, New York, N.Y. 10019) with a membership of 18,000 doctors, and the Gerontological Society's Clinical Medicine Section (1 Dupont Circle, Washington, D.C. 20036) may be able to help you locate doctors in your area who are interested in geriatrics. You can also write the Office of Information of the National Institute on Aging or the National Institute of Mental Health (Bethesda, Maryland 20014) for a list of persons or clinics specializing in geriatrics and gerontology arranged by geographical area.

Remember, however, that there is an extremely small percentage of doctors active in this field. It is also true that membership in these organizations does not guarantee competence in the field of aging, and individual doctors who are not specialists in the field may be equally sensitive and knowledgeable in working with older people. An able and understanding general practitioner or internist who takes care of patients of all ages can serve you very well indeed. If you are lucky, your own doctor may be such a person. Some people, of course, feel more comfortable talking about sexual problems with a new doctor who is a total stranger, and if this is the case with you, by all means do so. The main point is to go to a doctor with whom you feel as relaxed as possible and whom you trust to be both medically competent and generally receptive toward older people.

What else can you do? You owe it to yourself to learn how to give proper information and ask the right questions, and thus encourage your doctor to take your sexual problems seriously. It may be embarrassing to talk about what is on your mind. Don't let that stop you. Your experiences and problems are shared by many older people. Tell the doctor exactly what you are worried about. Include every detail that you think might be helpful in evaluating the symptoms. (If you have a hearing problem, be sure to ask the doctor to speak loudly enough for you to hear clearly.) Older women may feel reluctant to describe sexual problems in general, or problems in the vaginal area in particular, especially to a male doctor. Older men may not want to admit problems with potency. But this is false modesty and false pride. Tell all. Candid talk will go a long way toward making it easier to diagnose and treat your problem. The doctor's job is to help you, not judge you.

Your general practitioner or internist may recommend that you see a medical specialist, or you may decide this yourself. Gynecologists specialize in the genital problems of women. Many older women have rarely, if ever, had a thorough gynecological examination, but they will discover that there is little difficulty once they overcome their anxiety about lying on an examining table and allowing a doctor to examine their breasts carefully and conduct a painless internal or pelvic examination. This includes spreading the vaginal walls with an instrument called a speculum and palpating (examining with the hand) the internal female organs (the uterus, ovaries and surrounding ligaments) and abdomen. Urologists are specialists in the genito-urinary organs of men and the urinary organs (bladders) of women. Occasionally it may be necessary to consult an endocrinologist to evaluate the glandular system of the body, including the sex glands and the pituitary gland (the master gland in the brain) that regulates them.

There are a number of things you should look for as you work with doctors:

• Watch out for doctors who quickly dismiss your sexual concerns by saying, "What do you expect at your age?" "Go home and take a cold shower," "Stop worrying," "Nothing can be done." Persist in your desire for help, and if the doctor continues to be unresponsive, find a new doctor.

• Expect the doctor to take a good medical history, which includes a review of the body's systems and functions as well as a history of present and past illnesses. Specifically, the doctor should ask you about any changes you have observed in your genital organs, including in men any bowing of the penis and in women stress incontinence.

• Be aware that not only do diseases affect sexuality but that the proper control of disease may restore good sexual functioning in many instances.

• Expect the doctor to take a thorough sexual and marital history as well as a medical history. Questions are likely to include the ways you and your partner feel about sex, its frequency and pleasure, and about any disagreements you may have. He will also explore the impact of attitudes toward sex you may have developed in childhood. You will find it valuable to share with him the history of sexual experiences you may have had with other people at other times.

• The doctor should ask what drugs you are taking, both prescription and over-the-counter, and be able to explain the sexual side effects of each drug. It is sometimes possible to switch to equally effective drugs with fewer sexual side effects.

• If you have already had surgery on any sex organs, the doctor should be able to tell you if this is in any way affecting your sexuality. If surgery is planned, learn in advance any possible sexual consequences. Do not be embarrassed to ask specific questions about anything that is troubling you.

• Discuss with your doctor a program of preventive health care. This should include attention to smoking, drinking, nutrition, exercise, rest, stress and emotional problems.

• If you feel your doctor's examination has been insufficient, using these questions and the doctor's reactions to you as a guide and relying as well on your own common sense, talk to him or her openly about your misgivings. As a patient you are entitled to satisfaction.

After the medical examination it should be fairly clear whether physical problems are the sole or, more likely, the partial cause of symptoms of sexual dysfunction and whether medical treatment is indicated. In the majority of cases, the medical examination is likely to show that bodily changes are not involved, significantly or at all, and the search for the causes of sexual problems must move to emotional or psychological areas.

Psychological Help. Most sexual problems have emotional components, even when the original cause is physical. Others are entirely emotional in origin. Much of what we have said about the competence and inclinations of medical doctors with regard to older people holds true for psychotherapists and counselors. They tend to be unaware of and at times uninterested in the emotional problems of later life. They have usually had some training in sex education but rarely in the specialized area of sex after sixty. To find a therapist who can be of help to you will likely require determination.

There are several types of therapy to choose from. *Individual psychotherapy* means talking with a therapist one-to-one, on a regular basis. *Marital counseling* involves both you and your spouse. A broader term is *couples therapy,* which encompasses unmarried couples as well. *Family counseling* includes other members of your family. *Psychoanalysis* is an intensive form of individual psychotherapy, requiring several sessions per week. *Group psychotherapy* usually consists of a group of five to ten patients whose problems are discussed by the group under the guidance of one or two therapists. *Sex therapy* is a relatively new specialty which concentrates on the actual sexual problem itself, teaching couples how to make love more effectively.

The background and training of therapists vary greatly. Psychotherapists can be *psychiatrists* (M.D.'s who specialize in psychiatry), *psychologists* (masters or Ph.D.'s in psychology) or *social workers* (with masters' or doctoral degrees in social work).* *Psychoanalysts* are psychiatrists with advanced training in the psychoanalytic method. All these fields require a program of formal education and a supervised training period in psychotherapy or case work. All states require doctors to be licensed, and this is beginning to be true for practicing psychologists and social workers as well. Social workers who are certified (you will see the letters ACSW — for Academy of Certified Social Workers — after their names) by the National Association of Social Workers have had a period of professional training and examination beyond the master's degree.

In addition to psychotherapists there are numerous other kinds of counselors. *Marriage counselors* work with marriage and sex problems. This is a still unregulated field and practitioners range from competent and well-trained professionals to quacks and charlatans. Be careful to investigate the credentials (professional training and experience) of anyone you are considering as a counselor.

---

*Social work is a confusing field since people may define themselves as social workers because of the kind of work they do rather than because of their training. Ask if the social worker has, at minimum, a master's degree in social work.

Pastoral counseling has grown out of the counseling role of clergymen, with individual clergymen giving counseling or supervising and training other clergymen and lay persons to counsel. Again the quality of this counseling depends on the individual training and skills of each clergyman, since there are no standard requirements for such training in theological schools.

Therapists calling themselves *sex counselors* have proliferated in the past few years, following Masters and Johnson's important clinical work in the treatment of sexual dysfunction. It is estimated that three to five thousand sex clinics and individual counselors now offer such therapy. Many are frightfully expensive and the therapists are untrained. Masters and Johnson contend that fewer than fifty sex clinics are staffed by well-trained and competent sex-therapy teams. Because this is a new and unregulated field, without an organized structure of qualifications, requirements, examinations, clinical experience or peer review — and because sexual problems are so susceptible to exploitation by skillful, smooth-talking incompetents — the choice of a sex counselor requires very careful consideration. Watch out for quacks. They are likely to do more harm than good.

How do you find competent psychotherapists and counselors? Some sources to check are university medical schools and clinical teaching hospitals; local medical or psychiatric societies; university schools of social work; community mental health centers; senior centers; local chapters of the National Association of Social Workers (write to 600 Southern Building, Fifteenth and H Streets, N.W., Washington, D.C. 20005); the American Psychological Association* (1200 Seventeenth Street, N.W., Washington, D.C. 20036); the National Association for Mental Health, with 950 chapters in the United States (1800 North Kent Street, Arlington, Virginia 22209); the

---

*Direct your inquiries specifically to either the APA's Clinical Psychology Division or the Division of Adult Development and Aging, lest you get lost in one of their many other divisions.

Family Service Association of America (44 East Twenty-third Street, New York, N.Y. 10010) or their member Family Service agencies; and your family doctor and clergyman. Be specific and ask for a therapist who will be interested in working with an older person in sex counseling. Ask for at least two names so you will be able to make a choice. Friends and acquaintances may be able to refer you to professionals who have been helpful to them, as long as you recognize that individual preferences vary considerably.

The National Institute of Mental Health's Center on Aging (5600 Fishers Lane, Rockville, Maryland 20052) and the Gerontological Society's Social Research, Planning and Practice Section (1 Dupont Circle, Washington, D.C. 20036) can be contacted for information. The American Association of Marriage and Family Counselors (225 Yale Avenue, Claremont, California 91711) is pressing for regulation of persons who call themselves marriage counselors and should be able to refer you to someone in your locale (including Canada). The American Association of Sex

Educators and Counselors (5010 Wisconsin Avenue, N.W., Suite 304, Washington, D.C. 20016) certifies sex counselor-therapists and has a national roster from which names can be obtained. You may want to write Masters and Johnson for referral to competent sex counselors near you who have been trained by them (William H. Masters, M.D., and Virginia E. Johnson, Reproductive Biology Research Foundation, 4910 Forest Park Boulevard, St. Louis, Missouri 63108). The Sex Information and Education Council of the United States (SIECUS), 122 East Forty-second Street, New York, N.Y. 10017, is an additional source of information and referral.

The cost of therapy varies from free clinics and free counseling to sliding fees based on income, up to costs, in 1975, of $40 to $60 per fifty-minute session. Group therapy is less costly than individual therapy, ranging from $15 to $20 per one-and-one-half-hour session. Some health insurance plans partially cover costs of psychotherapy. Most do not. Medicare allows only $250 per year for outpatient psychotherapy, and only if performed by a psychiatrist. No insurance program covers sex therapy per se.

The amount of time required for evaluating and, if possible, resolving a particular sexual problem varies. Sometimes a single session can be enough. More often a series of weekly sessions is recommended, lasting from several months to more than a year, or, in the case of psychoanalysis, a number of years. Intensive two-week programs in sex therapy are offered by Masters and Johnson, with a five-year follow-up. The cost in 1975 was $2,500, with 30 percent of the patients receiving lowered fees or free care, based on income.

What Happens in Psychotherapy? You will tell about and explore your past patterns, your lifetime habits of living. You can't literally change the past, obviously, but you can gain perspective about it, change the way you feel about it, and break old habits and acquire new ways of coping effectively. For example, you will be helped to understand the sources of sexual problems you may have, lose certain inhibitions and learn new avenues of sexual expression. Therapeutic counseling does not simply dwell on the past, however. You will be discussing the here and now, your present relationships, always looking for your *own* responsibility for what is happening in your life. You will be asked questions, comments will be made (some may startle you) and suggestions may be proposed. Working out conflicts and going in new directions, therefore, comes about through joint work by you *and* your therapist on the past and the present. You work together on your private life. The process may remind you of both parenting and teaching. You retain your basic personality, but hopefully you rid yourself of unwelcome symptoms, gain insight and enhanced well-being, and increase your effectiveness in everyday living. Altogether you are likely to feel better about yourself.

How should you act when you go to the therapist? Once again, be frank. Tell him or her whatever is troubling you. There are certain basic things you can require or expect:

• Your therapist needs to be well informed both about the problems of older people and about sexual problems. Don't be afraid to question therapists about their background, training and general interest in these areas. Evaluate their answers (or failures to answer) in terms of what you now know — from this book and from your own experiences — to be important to you.

• The therapist should ask for your sexual, marital and personal history, and probably will want a medical report from your doctor.

• You should feel a sense of rapport and comfort with the therapist by the time you have had several sessions. If not, talk over your feelings frankly. If matters do not improve, you may need to consider a different therapist since rapport and trust are crucial to working effectively on sexual and emotional problems. Do not consider the need to change therapists the result of a flaw in yourself. Each individual's requirements in a relationship as close as that of therapist and patient will be different, and intangible but crucial factors like empathy, perception, manner and attitude are involved in making the right choice. A personality and approach that are right for one person may be all wrong for another. As long as you are candid in your encounters with the therapist, you can trust your perceptions about whether he or she is a good choice for you.

As for your part in therapy, you must learn:

- to set aside shyness and embarrassment;
- to open your mind and feelings to new ideas and insights;
- to be willing to actively try new directions in your relationships with others;
- to realize that while many things can improve, some things cannot. Once you have decided which is which, with the aid of the therapist, you then can begin to take advantage of those areas where improvement can realistically occur.

Even sexual problems that have existed for many years can sometimes be resolved. Masters and Johnson have declared optimistically: "The fact that innumerable men and women have not been sexually effective before reaching their late fifties or early sixties is no reason to condemn them to continuing sexual dysfunction as they live out the rest of their lifespan. The disinclination of the medical and behavioral professions to treat the aging population for sexual dysfunction has been a major disservice perpetrated by these professions upon the general public."

Therefore, whether your sexual problems are new or long-term, as long as they are troubling to you, you owe it to yourself to see what can be done to resolve them. In many cases you will be rewarded with surprisingly good results.

10

The Second Language of Sex

Can sex really remain interesting and exciting after forty, fifty or sixty years of adulthood? Older people themselves have testified that it can. Affection, warmth and sensuality do not have to deteriorate with age and may, in fact, increase.

Sex in later life is sex for its own sake: pleasure, release, communication, shared intimacy. Except for older men married to younger women, it is no longer associated with childbearing and the creation of families. This freedom can be both exhilarating and insightful, especially for those who have literally never had the time until now to think about and get to know themselves and each other.

Love and sex can mean many different things to older people. Some of them will be obvious to you; others less so:

• *The opportunity for expression of passion, affection, admiration, loyalty and other positive emotions.* This can occur in long-term relationships which have steadily grown and developed over the years, in relationships which actually improve in later years, and in new relationships such as second marriage.

• *An affirmation of one's body and its functioning.* Active sex demonstrates to older persons that their bodies are still capable of working well and providing pleasure. For many people, satisfactory sexual functioning is an extremely important part of their lives and helps to maintain high morale and enthusiasm.

• *A strong sense of self.* Sexuality is one of the ways people get a sense of their identity — who they are and their impact on others. Positive reactions from others preserve and enhance self-esteem. Feeling "feminine" or "masculine" is connected with feeling valued as a person. "I am now old" is quite different from feeling "I am older, and I can still see that others find me sexually appealing." Negative reactions depress and discourage older people and may tempt them to write off their sexuality forever.

• *A means of self-assertion.* The patterns of self-assertion available when people are young change as they grow older. Their children are grown-up and gone, their jobs are usually behind them. Personal and social relationships now become far more important as outlets for expressing personality. Sex can be a valuable means of positive self-assertion. One man told us, "I feel like a million dollars when I make love even though we are scrimping along on Social Security. My wife has always made me feel like a great success in bed and I believe I do the same for her. We've been able to stand a lot of stress in life because of our closeness this way."

• *Protection from anxiety.* The intimacy and the closeness of sexual union bring security and significance to people's lives, particularly when the outside world threatens them with hazards and losses. An older couple we know described the warmth of their sexual life as "a port in the storm," a place to escape from worry and trouble. Another older woman, aware of eventual death, called sex "the ultimate closeness against the night." Sex serves as a very important means of feeling in charge at a time when other elements of one's life tend to get out of control more frequently.

• *Defiance of the stereotypes of aging.* Familiar though they are with the derogatory attitudes of society toward late-life sex, older people who are sexually active defy the neutered status expected of them. We have had them say to us, "We're not finished yet," "I'm not ready to kick the bucket," "You can't keep a good man [woman] down," or "There may be snow on the roof but there's still fire in the furnace."

• *The pleasure of being touched or caressed.* Older widows and widowers tell us how much they now miss the simple pleasure and warmth of physical closeness, of being touched, held and caressed by someone they care for. Holding and hugging friends, children and pets offers some compensation but does not replace the special intimacy and feeling of being cared about that can exist in a good relationship or sexual union.

• *A sense of romance.* The courting aspects of sexuality may be highly significant — flowers, soft lights, music, a sense of romantic pursuit, elegance, sentiment and courtliness — and give pleasure in themselves. Romance may continue even when sexual intercourse, for various reasons, ceases. Mr. and Mrs. Denham, a couple in their eighties, described their evenings together to us. They typically bathe and dress for dinner, she in a long dress, he in a suit and tie. They dine with candlelight and music, and put the dishes aside until morning. They continue to listen to music from their record library during the evening, holding hands, chatting and enjoying each other's companionship. At bedtime they bid each other good night and fall asleep in each other's arms. Often they awaken in the middle of the night and have long, intimate conversations, sleeping late the next morning. Mr. Denham said of his wife, "I fall in love with her every day. My feelings grow stronger when I realize we have only a certain amount of time left.''

• *An affirmation of life.* Sex expresses joy and continued affirmation of life. The quality of one's most intimate relationships is an important measure of whether life has been worthwhile. An otherwise successful person may count his life a failure if he has been unable to achieve significant closeness to other persons, because he has never felt fully desired or accepted. Conversely, people with modest accomplishments may feel highly satisfied about themselves if they have been affirmed through intimate relationships. Sex is only one way of achieving intimacy, of course, but it is an especially profound affirmation of the worthwhileness of life.

• *A continuing search for sensual growth and experience.* Some older persons who find sex exciting and fascinating continue to search for ways to enhance it. Others are dissatisfied with their present sex lives and look for ways to improve them. Older people, as well as younger, seek marriage counseling, pursue divorces, remarry, or have affairs in the hope of finding what they are searching for. Many can find this growth and excitement within their present relationship.

Love and sex are twin arts requiring effort and knowledge. Only in fairy tales do people live happily ever after without working at it. It takes a continuous and active effort to master the processes which eradicate emotional distances between yourself and another. Responsibility toward another person as toward oneself is the golden rule of love. There is no motivation like truly caring for someone to encourage you to follow the rule. Add to this the knowledge, skills and time to cultivate a relationship, and love has a good chance of flourishing.

In studying older people Kinsey commented that those showing a decline in sexual interest seemed to be "affected by a psychological fatigue, a loss of interest in repetition of the same sort of experience, an exhaustion of the possibilities for exploring new techniques, new types of contacts, new situations." Apathy is epidemic among older persons in this country, not surprisingly, given the serious social, economic, health and personal problems so many of them must cope with. Drained and discouraged, many do elect to give up. But those who have continued to be, or have grown to become, lively and imaginative, despite their health, financial or other problems, are also numerous, and for them — as for you — personal relationships offer the richest of rewards.

When people are young and first getting used to sexuality, their sex tends to be urgent and explosive, involved largely with physical pleasure and in many cases the conception of children. This is the *first language of sex*. It is biological and instinctive, with wonderfully exciting and energizing potentialities. The process of discovering one's ability to be sexually desirable and sexually effective often becomes a way of asserting independence, strength, prowess and power. The first language of sex has been much discussed and written about because it is easy to study and measure — one can tabulate physical response, frequency of contacts, forms of outlet, sexual positions and physical skills in love-making. But sex is not just a matter of athletics and "production." Some young people recognize this early on and simultaneously develop a *second language of sex,* which is emotional and communicative as well as physical. Others continue largely in the first language — sometimes all their lives, sometimes only until they begin to see its limitations and desire something more.

The second language is largely learned rather than instinctive, and is often vastly underdeveloped since it depends upon your ability to recognize and share feelings in words, actions and unspoken perceptions, and to achieve a mutual tenderness and thoughtfulness between yourself and another person. In its richest form the second language becomes highly creative and imaginative, with bountiful possibilities for new emotional experiences. Yet it is a slow-developing art, acquired deliberately and painstakingly through years of experience in giving and receiving.

In the natural flow of events in the life cycle times will come when you may find yourself re-evaluating many areas of your life, including your sexuality. Middle age is the time when people typically begin to take stock of their lives and reassess their work, their personal relationships, their social and spiritual commitments. Retirement is another time when re-evaluations take place. Both periods can be chaotic, generating emotional upsets, divorce, higher risk of alcoholism and other evidences of stress.

But these can be constructive as well as dangerous ages, and the second language of sex has a good deal to offer you if you want to move in new directions in your personal life. Shared tenderness, warmth, humor, merriment, anger, passion, sorrow, camaraderie, fear — feelings of every conceivable sort can flow back and forth in a sexual relationship which has matured to this level of development.

Part of the secret of learning the second language lies in learning how to give. Receiving is much easier. It makes few demands. But the habit of only taking deadens the impulse to reciprocate. As Erich Fromm has said, "Most people see the problem of love primarily as that of being loved, rather than that of loving, of one's capacity to love." Giving is *not* an endless gift of yourself to others in which you expect nothing in return. Nor is it a marketplace transaction, trading with the expectation of an equal exchange. Healthy giving involves not only the hopeful and human anticipation that something equally good will be returned but also the pleasures inherent in giving, regardless of return. The balance to be struck must be chosen by each person and worked out in partnership.

The second language implies sensitivity. It means clearing up long-held grudges and old irritations toward your partner and people in general so your energy is not wasted in negativity. It suggests the possibility of renewing love every day. It requires knowing what pleases your partner and what pleases you. It involves playfulness as well as passion, and talking, laughing, teasing, sharing secrets, reminiscing, telling jokes, making plans, confessing fears and uncertainties, crying — in and out of the warmth of bed, in privacy and companionship. It need not always involve the sex act at all.

If boredom creeps into the relationship, both partners need to acknowledge it; it is time to look for or listen to the deeper feelings that each of you has hidden away against the time when the richness of such feelings will be welcome and restorative. You have to resist *actively* the pulls of habit. Routines and responsibilities may have dulled the impulse to really talk, and you must fight against succumbing to the temptation to withdraw into your own individual world. Self-centeredness, and wanting sexual and emotional contact only when you are in the mood, without concern for your partner's needs, is guaranteed to produce conflict. Competitiveness based on some fancied level of sexual performance is also deadly.

The second language of sex can be developed by *anyone willing to try*. Every day in our professional practice we see older people who have struggled courageously throughout their lives to overcome obstacles, to earn a living, raise a family, and carry out other responsibilities. In so doing they have literally sacrificed their private lives and individual growth to this process. No matter. Love and sex are *always* there to be rediscovered, enhanced or even appreciated for the very first time, whether you are young or very old. Self-starters have the advantage over those who wait passively for love to strike like lightning.

Older people have, in fact, a special ability to bring love and sex to new levels of development literally because they are older. They develop perceptions which are connected with the unique sense of having lived a long time and having struggled to come to terms with life as a cycle from birth to death. A number of these qualities are beautifully suited to the flourishing of the second language. An appreciation of the preciousness of life and the valuing of immediateness can occur as people become older. What counts now is the present moment, where once it was the casually expected future. If the growing awareness of the brevity of life leads you to come to terms with your own mortality in a mature and healthy way, no longer denying it, you will find you no longer live heedlessly, as though you had all the time in the world. The challenge of living as richly as possible in the time you have left is exhilarating, not depressing.

Elementality — the enjoyment of the elemental things of life — may develop in late life precisely because older people are more keenly aware that life is short. They tell us that they find themselves becoming adept in separating out the important from the trivial. Responsiveness to nature, human contact, children, music, to beauty in any form, may be heightened. Healthy late life is frequently a time for greater enjoyment of all the senses — colors, sights, sounds, smells, touch — and less involvement with the transient drives for achievement, possessions and power.

Older people have time for love. Although they have fewer years left to live than the young and middle-aged, if they are in reasonably good health, they can often spend more time on social and sexual relationships than any other age group. It is true that many have limited financial resources, but fortunately social and personal relationships are among the pleasures in life which can be free of charge.

Experience counts too. Many people *do* learn from experience. It is possible to become quite different in later life from what you were in youth. Obviously, the change can go in positive or negative directions. But the thing to remember is that change is possible. You do not need to become locked into any particular mode of behavior at any time of life. Experimentation and learning are possible all along the life cycle, and this holds true for sex and love. Naturally, the more actively you grow, the greater the reservoir of experience and the larger the repertoire you can draw upon in getting along with and loving other people. A man in his seventies gave this description of the bond between himself and his wife after forty-four years of marriage. "Sometimes I look at her in the morning and she does the same thing to me. We don't say anything, not even 'Good morning.' We understand each other. She is in bed when I get up and she'll look up and there are lots of things we don't have to say. 'You love me and I love you.' We have been married a long time and I think we understand each other.''

Perhaps only in the later years can life with its various possibilities have the chance to shape itself into something approximating a human work of art. And perhaps only in later life, when personality reaches its final stages of development, can love-making and sex achieve the fullest possible growth. Sex does not merely exist after sixty; it holds the possibility of becoming greater than it ever was. It can be joyful and creative, healthy and health-giving. It unites human beings in an affirmation of love and is therefore also morally right and virtuous. Those older persons who have no partners and must experience sex alone need to know that this, too, is their right — a healthy giving to oneself that reflects a strong sense of self-esteem and worth. Those who informed us as we wrote this book have given every one of us a valuable gift — a realistic expectation of sex after sixty.

Glossary

Androgen. Any of the *steroid** hormones produced by the adrenal glands and the *testes* that develop and maintain masculine characteristics; *testosterone* is the best known.

Anus. The opening from the lower bowel (colon) through which solid waste is passed.

Atrophy. A wasting away or diminution in size of a cell, tissue, organ, part or body.

Bartholin's glands. Two small, roundish bodies, one on each side of the vaginal opening. Although they produce mucus in sexual excitement, they are not the

*Words italicized are defined elsewhere in the Glossary.

primary source of vaginal lubrication during intercourse.

Benign prostatic hypertrophy (BPH). Noncancerous enlargement of the *prostate* gland that occurs in the middle and later years.

Bladder. The distendable elastic sac that serves as a receptacle and place of storage for the urine.

Cervix. The part of the *uterus,* sometimes called the neck, which protrudes into the *vagina.*

Circumcision. Surgical removal of the foreskin, a loose fold of skin that surrounds the head of the *penis.*

Climacteric. See **Menopause.**

Climax. See **Orgasm.**

Clitoris. A small, erectile organ at the upper end of the *vulva,* homologous with the *penis,* and a significant focus of sexual excitement and *orgasm* in the woman.

Coitus. Copulation, coition, sexual intercourse.

Cowper's glands. A pair of small glands lying alongside and discharging into the male *urethra.* They contribute lubrication during sexual activity.

Cystitis. Inflammation of the urinary bladder.

Dyspareunia. The occurence of pain in the sexual act, usually experienced in the female vaginal area.

Ejaculation. The forceful emission of the seminal fluid at *orgasm*.

Ejaculatory impotence. Inability to ejaculate.

Erogenous zones. Sensitive areas of the body, such as the mouth, lips, buttocks, breasts and genital areas, which are important in sexual arousal.

Estrogen. One of the active female hormones produced by the *ovaries* and the adrenal glands, which has a profound effect on the generative organs and breasts.

Fallopian tube. The tube that leads from each *ovary* into the *uterus;* after *ovulation* the ovum travels through the tube on its way to the *uterus* and fertilization takes place in the tube.

Flushes (or flashes), hot. A symptom associated with the hormonal changes during *menopause,* caused by a sudden rapid dilation of blood vessels.

Foreplay. Sexual acts which precede intercourse during which the partners stimulate each other by kissing, touching and caressing.

Frigidity. An imprecise term applied to various aspects of female sexual inadequacy: (1) popularly, abnormal lack of desire, or coldness; (2) inability to achieve an *orgasm* through intercourse; (3) inability to achieve orgasm by any means; (4) any other level of sexual response considered unsatisfactory by the woman or her partner.

Genital area. The area which contains the external genital organs such as the *vulva* in the female and the *penis* in the male.

Genitalia. The reproductive organs, especially the external organs.

Hormones. Chemical substances produced in the ductless (endocrine) glands of the body and discharged directly into the blood stream. They have specific effects upon the activity of a certain organ or organs. Sexual hormones regulate the entire reproductive cycle. (The body produces many nonsexual hormones as well.)

Hormone therapy. The medical use of supplementary hormones (other than or in addition to those produced by the endocrine glands) for treatment of diseases and deficiencies.

Impotence. Lack of erectile power in the male *penis,* which prevents copulation.

Labia. Two rounded folds of tissue that form the outer boundaries of the external genitals in the female.

Libido. Sexual desire.

Mastectomy. Surgical removal of a breast.

Masturbation. Stimulation of the sex organs, usually to *orgasm,* through manual or mechanical means.

Medical specialties regarding sex:

Endocrinology. The functions and diseases of the ductless (endocrine) glands.

Gynecology. The diseases, reproductive functions, organs and endocrinology of females.

Urology. The functions, organs and diseases of the urinary system in males and females and of the reproductive system in males.

Menopause. The time of life for the human

female, usually between the ages of 45 and 50, which is marked by the cessation of *menstruation* and *ovulation*. It may be gradual or sudden, and it can last from three months to three years, or even longer. It marks the end of childbearing potential.

Menstruation. The periodic discharge of body fluid (menses) from the *uterus* through the vagina, occurring normally about once a month.

Nocturnal emission. Ejaculation of *semen* at night while asleep; often called a wet dream.

Oral-genital sex. Forms of stimulation of the genitalia by the mouth:

Cunnilingus. Stimulation of vulva (especially the clitoris and labia) by the partner's mouth and tongue.

Fellatio. Stimulation of the penis by the partner's mouth and tongue.

Soixante-neuf (or **sixty-nine**). Simultaneous and mutual stimulation of the genitalia by the mouth and tongue by two partners of the same or opposite sex.

Orchidectomy (orchiectomy). Removal of

one or both *testes;* castration.

Orgasm. The culmination of the sex act. There is a feeling of sudden, intense pleasure accompanied by an abrupt increase in pulse rate and blood pressure. Involuntary spasms of pelvic muscles cause relief of sexual tension with vaginal contractions in the female and *ejaculation* by the male. It lasts up to ten seconds.

Ovaries. The two major reproductive glands of the female, in which the ova (eggs) are formed and *estrogen,* or female hormones, are produced.

Ovulation. The process in which a mature egg is discharged by an *ovary* for possible fertilization.

Papanicolaou smear (Pap smear) test. A simple test to determine the presence of cancer of the *uterus* by analyzing cells taken from the *cervix* or *vagina.*

Penis. The male organ of sexual intercourse.

Perineum. (1) The internal portion of the body in the pelvis occupied by urogenital passages and the rectum; (2) the internal and external region between the *scrotum* and *anus* in the man, and the *vulva* and *anus* in the woman.

Pituitary gland. An endocrine gland consisting of three lobes, located at the base of the brain. The body's "master gland," it controls the other endocrine glands and influences growth, metabolism and maturation.

Potency. Sexual capacity for intercourse; the ability to achieve and sustain erection. Applied only to the male.

Premature ejaculation. Almost instant *ejaculation* (within 3 seconds) upon entry of the *penis* into the *vagina*.

Prostate. A walnut-sized body, partly muscular and partly glandular, which surrounds the base of the urethra in the male. It secretes a milky fluid which is discharged into the *urethra* at the time of emission of *semen*.

Prostatectomy. Surgical removal of part or all of the *prostate*. There are three types, depending upon the anatomical approach: (1) transurethral (TUR); (2) suprapubic (or retropubic); and (3) perineal.

Prostatism, prostatitis. Inflammation or

congestion in the *prostate.*

Refractory period. See **sexual response cycle.**

Replacement therapy. See **hormone therapy.**

Scrotum. The sac containing the *testes.*

Semen. The whitish fluid containing sperm, which is discharged in *ejaculation.*

Sensuality. The wider aspect of *sexuality;* the involvement of all the physical senses that enhance and express one's sexuality.

Sex. (1) Urge for and (2) act of sexual union.

Sex hormones. See **hormones.** Sexual hormones regulate the entire reproductive cycle.

Sexual dysfunction. A general term for different varieties and degrees of unsatisfying sexual response and performance.

Sexual fantasies. Vivid and excitatory imaginings about sex; healthy and common in both sexes.

Sexual response cycle. The physical changes that occur in the body during sexual excitement and orgasm. It includes four phases: (1) the **excitement**

or erotic-arousal phase during foreplay; (2) the **intromission** or plateau phase; (3) the **orgasmic** or climax phase; and (4) the **resolution** or recovery phase. The time required for the completion of recovery — the time required before the first phase can be successfully initiated again — is called the **refractory** period. The refractory period is more critical to the male.

Sexuality. The emotional and physical responsiveness to sexual stimuli. Also, one's sexual identity, role and perception; one's femininity; one's masculinity.

Sperm. Spermatozoa, the male reproductive cells, produced by the *testes* and discharged during intercourse into the *vagina.*

Sterility. The incapacity to reproduce sexually; infertility.

Steroids. A class of chemical substances that includes the *sex hormones.*

Testes (testicles). The two male reproductive glands, located in the cavity of the *scrotum,* the source of spermatozoa and the androgens.

Testosterone. A male hormone (an *androgen*), a *steroid,* produced by the testes.

Thyroid gland. The gland partially surrounding the windpipe (trachea) in the neck whose function is to supply hormones which adjust the metabolism of the body.

Urethra. The passage or canal in the *penis* through which the male discharges both urine and *sperm.* In women the passage through which urine passes.

Urethritis. Inflammation of the *urethra.*

Urogenital system. The organs that serve the functions of urination, sexual activity and procreation.

Uterus (womb). The hollow muscular organ in the female in which the embryo and fetus develop to maturity.

Vagina. The tube or sheath leading from the *uterus* to the *vulva* at the exterior of the body. It receives the *penis* during intercourse.

Vaginitis. Inflammation of the *vagina.*

Vas deferens. The duct from each *testicle* that carries *sperm* to the *penis.*

Venereal disease. Any disease which is

transmitted during sexual intercourse.

Virility. Masculine vigor, including potency (from which it must be distinguished), sexual prowess (skill), sexual frequency and attractiveness.

Vulva. The external female genitalia, including the *labia, clitoris* and the outer *vagina.*

Womb. See **uterus.**

Recommended Reading

Books of General Interest

Clinebell, Howard J., and Clinebell, Charlotte. *The Intimate Marriage.* New York: Harper & Row, 1970.

Comfort, Alex. *The Joy of Sex.* New York: Crown Publishers, Inc., 1972.

Fromm, Erich. *The Art of Loving.* New York: Harper & Row, 1956.

Masters, William H., and Johnson, Virginia E. *Human Sexual Inadequacy.* Boston: Little, Brown and Company, 1970.

Miles, Herbert J. *Sexual Happiness in Marriage.* Grand Rapids, Mich.: Zondervan Publishing House, 1967.

If You Wish to Read Further

Bailey, Derrick S. *Sexual Relations in Christian Thought*. New York: Harper & Row, 1959.

Berezin, Martin S. "Sex and Old Age: A Review of the Literature," *Journal of Geriatric Psychiatry 2:*131 - 149, 1969.

Burnside, Irene M. "Sexuality and Aging," *Medical Arts and Sciences 27,* No. 3, 13 - 27, 1973.

Butler, Robert N. "Sex After 65," in *Quality of Life: The Later Years* (edited by Leo E. Brown and Effie O. Lewis). The American Medical Association. Acton, Mass.: Publishing Sciences Group, Inc., 1975.

Butler, Robert N., and Lewis, Myrna I. *Aging and Mental Health*. St. Louis: The C. V. Mosby Co., 1973.

Dean, Stanley R. "Sin and Social Security," *Journal of the American Geriatrics Society, 14:*935 - 38, 1966.

Dlin, Barney M., and Perlman, Abraham. "Emotional Response to Ileostomy and Colostomy in Patients over the Age of 50," *Geriatrics 26:*113 - 118, 1971.

Finkle, Alex L. "Sexual Function During

Advancing Age," Chapter 29 in *Clinical Geriatrics* (edited by I. Rossman). Philadelphia: J. B. Lippincott, 1971.

Ford, Clellan S., and Beach, Frank A. *Patterns of Sexual Behavior.* New York: Harper & Row, 1951.

Freeman, Joseph T. "Sexual Aspects of Aging," Chapter 13 in *The Care of the Geriatric Patient.* St. Louis: The C. V. Mosby Co., 1971.

Freeman, Joseph T. "John S. — Widower," *Journal of the American Geriatrics Society, 18:*736 - 746, 1970.

Group for the Advancement of Psychiatry. *Assessment of Sexual Function: A Guide to Interviewing.* New York: 1973.

Guild, W. *After Your Heart Attack.* New York: Harper & Row, 1969.

Hellerstein, H. E., and Friedman, E. H. "Sexual Activity and the Post Coronary Patient," *Archives of Internal Medicine. 125:*987, 1970. *Medical Aspects of Human Sexuality 3:*70, 1969.

Katchadourian, Herant A., and Lunde, D.T. *Fundamentals of Human Sexuality.* New York: Holt, Rinehart & Winston, 1972.

Kinsey, Alfred C.; Pomeroy, Wardell; and Martin, Clyde E. *Sexual Behavior in the Human Male*. Philadelphia: The W. B. Saunders Co., 1948.

Kinsey, Alfred C.; Pomeroy, Wardell; Martin, Clyde E.; and Gebhard, Paul M. *Sexual Behavior in the Human Female*. Philadelphia: The W. B. Saunders Co., 1955.

Lewis, Myrna I., and Butler, Robert N. "Why Is Women's Lib Ignoring Older Women?," *Aging and Human Development 3*:223 - 231, 1972.

McKain, Walter C. *Retirement Marriage*. Storrs, Conn.: University of Connecticut, 1969.

Masters, William H., and Johnson, Virginia E. *Human Sexual Response*. Boston: Little, Brown and Co., 1966.

Newman, Gustave, and Nichols, Claude R. "Sexual Activities and Attitudes in Older Persons," *Journal of American Medical Association 173*:33 - 35, 1960.

Pfeiffer, Eric; Vervoerdt, Adriaan; and Wang, Hsioh-Shan. "The Natural History of Sexual Behavior in Aged Men and Women," *Archives of General Psychiatry 19*:753 - 758, 1968.

The President's Council on Physical Fitness and Sports and the Administration on Aging. *The Fitness Challenge in the Later Years: An Exercise Program for Older Americans.* DHEW Publication No. (OHD/AOA) 73 - 20802, 1968. Reprinted 1973.

Rubin, Isadore. *Sexual Life After Sixty.* New York: Signet Books, 1965.

Rubin, Isadore. *Sexual Life in the Later Years.* New York: SIECUS (Sex Information and Education Council of the United States), Study Guide No. 12, 1970.

Scheingold, Lee D., and Wagner, Nathaniel N. *Sex and the Aging Heart.* New York: Pyramid Books, 1975.

Shelmire, Bedford. *The Art of Looking Younger.* New York: St. Martin's Press, 1973.

Thewlis, Malford W. "Some Remarks on the History and Bibliography of Geriatrics," Chapter 1 in *The Care of the Aged (Geriatrics)*. St. Louis: The C. V. Mosby Co., 1954.

Veno, M. "The So-called Coital Death," *Japanese Journal of Legal Medicine 17*: 535, 1963.

Index

Friedman, E. H., 47
Frigidity, 154
Fromm, Erich, 243
Frustration, 48

Geriatrics, 215
Gerontological Society, 215
Gout, 128
Gray Panthers, 172, 195
Greenblatt, Robert, 66n
Grief, 103 - 106
Group psychotherapy, 222, 227
Guilt, 11, 14, 49, 109 - 111
Gynecological examination, 28 - 29, 113, 217 - 218

Hair care, 142 - 143
Hearing problems, 134 - 136
Heart disease, 44 - 50, 125 - 126
Hellerstein, H. E., 47
Hellerstein's Sexercise Tolerance Test, 47
Hernia, 56 - 57
Homosexuality, 190 - 191
Honeymoon cystitis, 22, 30
Hormones
    androgen, 17, 40
    estrogen, 18 - 29, 60
    replacement therapy, 21, 25 - 29, 66
    testosterone, 39, 66
Hypertension, 50
Hypogonadism, 66
Hysterectomy, 60, 70 - 72

Ideal Marriage (Van de Velde), 162

271